WITNESSES
TO WAR

WITNESSES
TO WAR

Personal documents of the
Anglo-Boer War from the collections
of the South African Library

SELECTED AND EDITED BY

KAREL SCHOEMAN

HUMAN & ROUSSEAU

CAPE TOWN PRETORIA JOHANNESBURG

Title page: 'Rebel D. Thom leaving Beaufort West': an undated snapshot from the Barrett Albums, showing a man shaded by a large umbrella proceeding down Donkin Street with a military guard, presumably under arrest. Note especially the nursemaid with the pram on the left. (INIL 2682)

FIRST EDITION, FIRST IMPRESSION 1998
SECOND IMPRESSION 1999

COPYRIGHT © 1998 BY KAREL SCHOEMAN
FIRST PUBLISHED IN 1998 BY
HUMAN & ROUSSEAU (PTY) LTD
STATE HOUSE, 3-9 ROSE STREET, CAPE TOWN
LAYOUT AND DESIGN BY CHÉRIE COLLINS
TYPESET IN 11.5 ON 14 PT BERKELEY
BY HUMAN & ROUSSEAU
PRINTED AND BOUND BY NATIONAL BOOK PRINTERS,
DRUKKERY STREET, GOODWOOD, WESTERN CAPE

ISBN 0 7981 3848 3

PREFACE

B ecause of the scale of the operations, their effect on the country as a whole and the number of people involved, a large number of documents relating to the Anglo-Boer War have inevitably found their way to the South African Library, where they are widely scattered over many collections and often hidden in obscure places. They include letters, diaries, reports, official as well as unofficial, a certain amount of printed material, printed and other ephemera, scrapbooks, cartoons, photographs and photograph albums, many of which have been described over the years in articles in the Library's *Quarterly Bulletin*.

The present publication is an anthology containing a random personal selection from this material; it is intended in the first place to illustrate the wide range of documents in the Library's holdings, and secondly to give an impression of the war as experienced by those who lived through it. The writings of the famous or prominent have as far as possible been avoided and an attempt has been made to provide due representation of the civilian population, especially the women.

Given the state of South African society at the time, relatively few records, unfortunately, were compiled by members of any of the non-white groups in the country, and of these few have survived, at any rate in the collections of the Library.

The intention of this book is not to gather together 'highlights of the war', nor has any attempt been made to assemble records of dramatic, exciting or ostensibly important events: for most of the people involved, it must be remembered, the war was not a matter of heroics, but of continuing their ordinary lives as best they could in extraordinary circumstances. To Antonia Corelli Green, writing from Pretoria just after the outbreak of war, the teething problems of her baby were in their way as significant as the expulsion of the Anglican Bishop or the Boer invasion of Natal, and Johanna Hendriksz, going out into the garden to listen to the first shells falling on the besieged Kimberley, noted, 'All was calm then, but the locusts are packed in the garden, awful things they are.'

In spite of subsequent attempts to dramatise or glamorise the events of the war, drama and excitement were in actual fact relatively scarce, and for the greater part, and for the majority of those involved, it was a time of boredom, frustration, futility and physical discomfort, of separation, disruption and destruction, difficulties of transport and supply, dysentery, blisters, dust, mud, flies and lice, against a constant background of actual or potential violence and danger.

The items appearing here have been arranged in a broadly chronological order. Each document transcribed is provided with a brief introduction giving some information on the writers and their situation, and further essential information is provided in the form of footnotes. As much has been explained as seems necessary to make the texts accessible to the general reader, but no attempt has been made to explain every reference made.

Documents in Dutch have been reproduced as written so as not to intrude unnecessarily between the original writer and the reader, but translations are given in the appendix on pp. 150-162. In these cases, proper names misspelled in the originals have been corrected in the translation and footnotes are provided with the latter when required.

Where possible each letter or diary entry has been quoted in its entirety, placing whatever incidents it describes in a wider context. Some editing has been done, mainly as regards capitalization, punctuation, paragraph divisions and writing out of abbreviations in full. Incidental misspellings have been corrected in transcription, except in cases where these form part of the writer's individual style, in which case it has been noted that the text is reproduced without change.

While I have tried to be as representative as possible in my selection, I have of course been limited by the range of material available to me. The fact that so much of the material used relates to the Free State Republic reflects in this particular case the emphasis in the collections, not my personal interests or preferences. Opinions expressed in the connecting text and the notes are, however, my own and not those of the Library.

The texts used come from material which has been donated to or purchased by the Library without any known restrictions on its use. There are, however, many collections which have no indication of provenance, and some material is held only in the form of photocopies, the whereabouts of the original texts being unknown; in many cases the material concerned was donated to the Library twenty or thirty years ago or more, and it has proved impossible to trace the original donors. In compiling this anthology, the Library has where this appeared necessary attempted to obtain the requisite permission for reproduction; in the absence of recorded restrictions or conditions it has acted in good faith, on the assumption that in acquiring the material it is has by implication also acquired authority to determine its further use, and no existing rights have been knowingly infringed.

The illustrations used in the book are not necessarily connected with the documents with which they appear, but are intended to provide a general visual background to the texts. They have also been taken from sources in the Library, which include contemporary journals, newspapers and books as well as original photographs in the picture collection. The weekly edition of the *Cape Times* has proved to be an especially valuable source of unique photographic material which has never been properly utilised, and it may be mentioned in passing that the Library has a card index to all illustrations appearing in this newspaper and its contemporary, the *Cape Argus Weekly*, over the period 1892-1902.

South African Library   KAREL SCHOEMAN
28 October 1997

CONTENTS

ACKNOWLEDGMENTS

I would like to record my gratitude to Jill Martin for her tactful editing; to Linette Viljoen and Chérie Collins of Human & Rousseau; to Jackie Loos and Penny Sonnenberg of the Picture Collection, South African Library; and to Enver Ebrahim of the Photographic Section for the high quality of the copy prints made by him for this book.

1.(opposite). The first British prisoners arrive at Pretoria station from Natal, October 1899 (detail). (PHA)

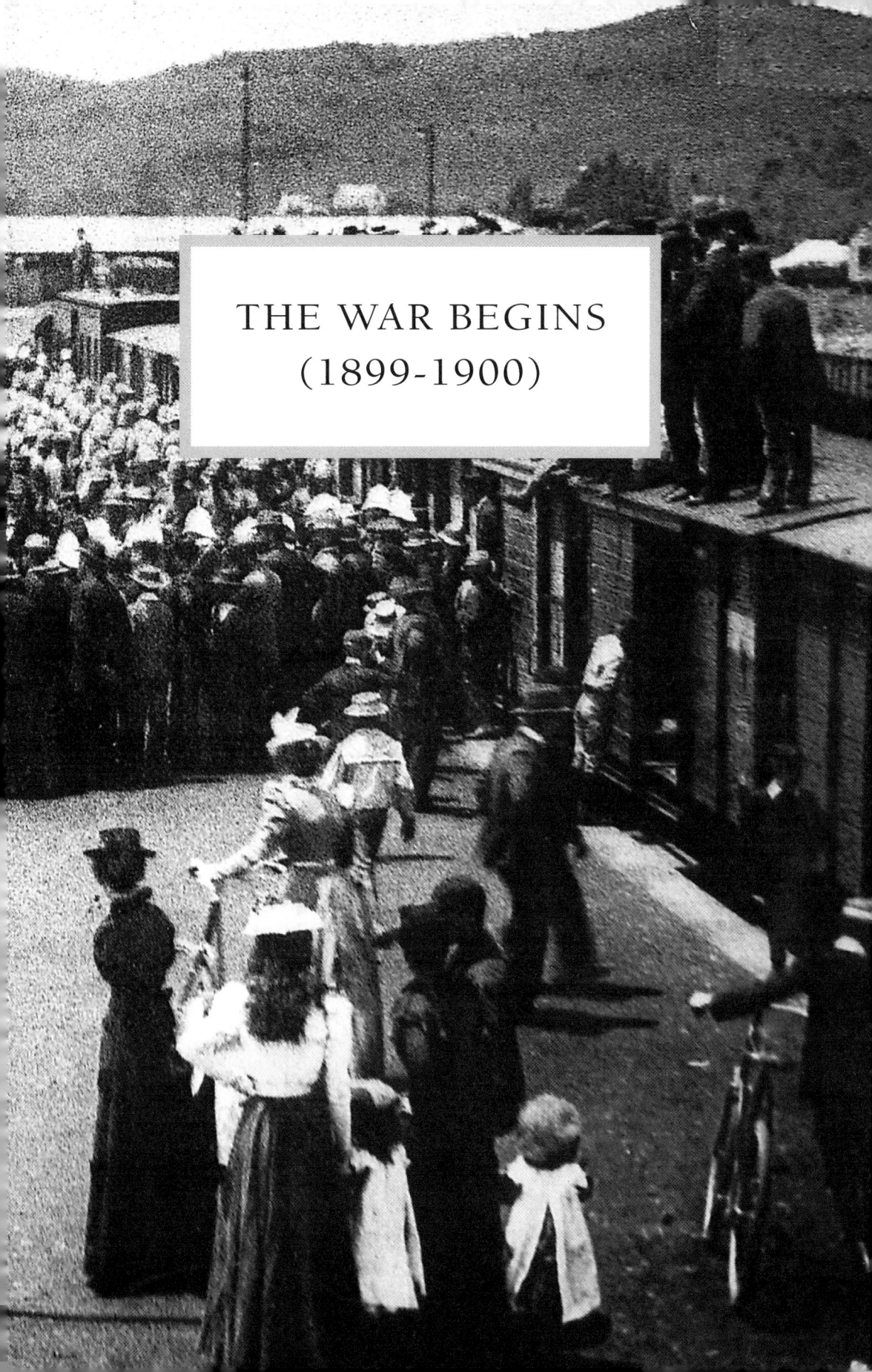

THE WAR BEGINS
(1899-1900)

*T*he Anglo-Boer War may be said to have begun with Jameson's unsuccessful invasion of the Transvaal Republic at the end of 1895.

For the remainder of the decade, events in South Africa were dominated increasingly by what the newspapers of the day called 'the situation'. In spite of the exchange of letters and diplomatic notes, formal negotiations, informal discussions behind the scenes and a last-minute meeting between President Kruger and Sir Alfred Milner in the winter of 1899, war between Great Britain and the Transvaal was inevitable. Active preparations for it had in fact begun on both sides almost immediately after the Raid.

In December 1895 the British garrison in South Africa numbered no more than 3588 officers and men, but it was enlarged steadily over the following years, and by October 1899 it had reached a total of no less than 22 104. In stationing these troops, the northern part of Natal, which was open to invasion from both the Orange Free State and Transvaal, received special attention, and more than half of the British forces in South Africa were initially placed here, among them the 5th (Royal Irish) Lancers.

J.B. Jardine, a lieutenant in this regiment since 1892, saw service for the full duration of the war: the first of his letters to his mother is reproduced below, and the last (written in Namaqualand in May 1902) on pp. 142-143 below. The letters were subsequently typed out on heavy paper and bound in quarter leather with gilt edging, which may indicate the pride the author himself took in this episode in his life. Whatever the background, however, Jardine's letters, written from a variety of places all over the country, are full and lively, and several of them have been included in this anthology.

Pietermaritzburg, 28th September 1899

Dearest Mother, – I am handing over the Remount business tomorrow, in order to reach the Regiment on the march at Colenso. I am sorry to give it up, as it is interesting work, but as war may break out at any moment, I should stand the chance of not being in the spot with the Regiment.

In my letter to Father I have explained the last move. It was very smartly done, as the Dublin Fusiliers and Leicestershires were warned at 7 p.m. and were off at 2 a.m. for Glencoe, where they arrived to the astonishment of the inhabitants. Today I hear they have thrown up the entrenchments, so you can well imagine we are on the very verge of war.

2. *Harriet Road, Pietermaritzburg, at the time of the Anglo-Boer War: the rural outskirts of a colonial town at the turn of the century, with trees, rickshas and a considerable number of pedestrians.* (INIL 3816)

I am going to apply for extra pay of 5/- per diem for the last three months. It is seldom during that time that I have got away any day before 5 p.m., which of course meant no polo, and I am including Sundays.

I hear our transport broke down yesterday owing to the heavy state of the roads, it having rained a great deal; a great object lesson to the authorities at home if they could hear of it. As I have said all along, we should be at them *now*. This delay is most disastrous. Another three weeks and the true rains will have begun, when the roads become morasses and the grass grows up for the Boer ponies. We don't know how long this campaign will last, but by the end of December horse-sickness will be rife, and one can easily foretell the results.

I met the Johannesburg train to-night at the station and it was crammed, as was also the part of the station behind the barriers with onlookers. The line passes our stables before it reaches the station, and the occupants of the trains always cheer frantically and wave handkerchiefs to the men as they pass. I am sorry for the married people; Mrs Parker, Mrs King and Mrs Graham are sharing a home while the operations take place. They are in an awful state, and when the Regiment marched out they did not put in an appearance.

At Ladysmith they have outposts every night now, and the roads towards the

11

Free State are patrolled in the early morning. It is quite on the cards that an attack will be made on it any day now, as there is only C Squadron of ours, the 69th of Battery and the Liverpools in camp there now. You see, it is only six hours' ride from Van Reenen's Pass. I rather think the move on Glencoe was with the object of protecting the Dundee coal-fields, as well as of making room behind for the Indian troops.

I have written to the agent to send the Mauser pistol to Ladysmith instead of here, as it cannot get here until I have left. The unfortunate Hooper is left behind to look after things with 12 men and 2 sergeant-majors, he being the junior man. I don't think we shall be long in Ladysmith; at any rate we will move to Newcastle as soon as an Indian regiment is ready to take our place, and the first arrives at Durban on the 4th proximo.

We all felt like two-year-olds in a furlong race when the starter will not drop his flag.

Best love from your ever affectionate son, J.B. Jardine.

Given the complexity of South African society, the prospect of war with all the divisions it implied inevitably led to conflicting demands on the loyalties of many people and caused much pain and distress. How mixed local loyalties often were, and in what unexpected ways people reacted to the challenge of the times, may be seen from a letter by Sarah Leith, a member of the Searle family of Great Brak River, who had been born in South Africa as the daughter of English immigrants. In 1886 she married a Scottish teacher, Thomas Leith, who subsequently took up a post at Heilbron in the Free State; in 1897 he was appointed housemaster at Grey College in Bloemfontein, with which he was to be closely associated for the remainder of his career. The Leiths had been living in the Free State for only five years, and their undemonstrative sense of duty is a testimony to the remarkable loyalty the Free State Republic was in its later days able to call forth even from English-speaking residents.

Charles Searle, to whom Mrs Leith was writing, was her brother; his 'fighting bravely for what you think is right' probably refers to the fact that he was at the time a member of the Cape House of Assembly, representing George. The 'boys' were boarders at Grey College, and 'Tom' was in the first case her husband, Thomas Leith, and in the second her brother, Thomas Searle; the other references have not been traced.

Grey College, Bloemfontein, Oct. 4th 1899

My dear Charles, – Just a note, as we may not be able to write very much longer. We do not know what a day may bring forth now.[1] Oh, I do hope there will be no

1. A scriptural quotation: 'Boast not thyself of tomorrow; for thou knowest not what a day may bring forth'; Prov. 27:1.

3. *Sarah Leith, née Searle, wife of Thomas Leith, headmaster of Grey College, Bloem-*
fontein; a studio portrait by Deale Brothers of Bloemfontein. (Searle Album 3)

war. It is such a miserable, hopeless prospect. We were glad to get your letter. We very often speak of you and think of you. You are fighting bravely for what you think is right. It is not nice to be abused and misrepresented, but public men expect that, and I know it does not trouble you over much.

We are passing through a terribly trying time. There are so many false rumours flying about that one is kept in a constant ferment. Our boys are constantly coming and going. It makes me so sad to think of our boys going to war, and how many will we see back! Some are such splendid fellows, and we are very fond of them.

We sent Miss Gregory and the children away last Friday. We miss them terribly, but it is so nice to know that they will have a pleasant time whatever we may have to put up with. Miss Lawrence is staying with me. Miss Gregory was very unwilling to go, but she is not strong and her people are so anxious about her that we did not care to have the responsibility of keeping her here. Besides, the boys will all leave if war unfortunately does come, and there will be very little work in the College, for already there is great distress. We are getting up entertainments to get money for a 'Relief Fund'.

Mother is anxious about us naturally and would like us to leave, but of course we have never thought such a thing for a moment. We could not be so mean as to leave the State in trouble when we have shared in its prosperity. Things are so terribly mixed and there seems so much wrong on both sides that there is no comfort anywhere.

Tom has been very, very busy since six o'clock Monday morning. He was commandeered to go round commandeering goods from the stores and different people. It was not a pleasant job – especially as it was the President's birthday and a holiday. It was so difficult to find people.

Tom was actually put down for 'active service', but Mr Elliott who was writing up the list got them to put him down for this work instead. It seems a great farce to commandeer townspeople for active service, many of whom have never fired a shot and can't ride a horse properly. Mary will be glad to leave for home.

Love to Tom and greetings from us both. Your loving sister Sally.

Antonia Corelli Green found herself in much the same position in Pretoria after the beginning of hostilities. She had been born in England, like her husband, Robert Cottle Green, an early Transvaal pioneer, but they had lived in Pretoria since 1891; she was a music teacher, and had written and published six Christmas carols for children under the title Sent from the Transvaal. *Her husband being a Transvaal burgher, they remained in Pretoria after the outbreak of the war on 11 October 1899, and Mrs Green kept a kindergarten which was attended by the younger children of the Secretary of State, F. W. Reitz, among others. The South African Library holds a photocopy of the surviving portion of the diary kept by her during the early months of the war.*

On 21 October, during the initial advance of the Boers into Natal, they had been sharply checked at Elandslaagte, where Dr Herman Coster of the Hollander Corps was killed and A.F. Schiel of the German Corps wounded and captured: this explains the first diary entry quoted. Dundee was occupied by the Boers two days later, and the battle of Ladysmith took place on 30 October. Bob was the writer's husband, Robert Cottle Green, and further references in the following extracts are to Anglican church affairs.

Tuesday, 24 [October 1899]. This is a dreadful time! War is raging, and such anxiety is felt here for friends and relatives. Poor Mr and Mrs Minaar have lost their boy (so report says), and what terrible grief must be in that house! A promising lad about eighteen shot down on the battle field! Dr Coster is also said to be dead, leav-

4. *Church Square, Pretoria, with the Government Buildings (right) and the Grand Hotel, from a snapshot taken shortly after the war by the visiting Quaker Lionel Richardson.* (INIL 10436)

ing a wife and three little children. Capt. Schiel is supposed to have died today from a wound. I just mention names known in Pretoria or among our friends.

All our clergy have been sent out of the Transvaal except Mr Godfrey, and I am temporary organist in the Cathedral. I played last Sunday morning and evening, the morning went swimmingly, but in the evening they gave me a boy that could not blow the organ properly, and oh how I suffered!

The prisoners were brought in on Sunday morning and are now in tents on the race course, 243 in number.

On last Wednesday night I went with Mrs Ferris, Miss Rorke, the Blackmores, &c. to see the Bishop and Mrs Bousfield off. Mr Matthews also left then, and the train was packed, cattle trucks *full* of people as well. It was late in starting, so about 10:30 we said good by and came home. I told the Bishop all of us who remained after the war would come to meet him on his return! He and Mrs Bousfield felt being turned out dreadfully.

Bob was 'on duty' that evening and could not see them. We both went to the Communion service that morning and saw Mr Matthews ordained a priest. Bob reads the Lessons in the Cathedral now and hands the plate round, and is head layman.

The same night the Bishop left we saw a big cannon at the station ready to

15

5. 'Last sitting, (. . .) Commission for the protection of Pretoria and preservation of peace and order from Oct. 4/99 to June 3/00.' Note especially the coloured attendant at the back (centre), and the electric lamps. (MSB 866,1(7))

leave for the front at 3 o'clock the next morning, and several burghers ready to go too. It looked awful standing there in the dark, and oh, how many English may be even now shot by it!

We hear sad reports on *this* side of the border about the English soldiers' behaviour. They are always reported to be running away! Three shots from a cannon and the white flag goes up! &c., &c., surely it cannot be true. Here the news is so one-sided.

This morning Bessie Reitz came in to tell me that *seven* English cannons were captured! and Dundee is supposed to be taken by the Boers. The English and Boers are at war in Ladysmith. A big battle [is] supposed to have been fought there.

Baby has been so poorly cutting two double teeth with diarrhoea, I had Dr Fehrsen in yesterday, but I think the sweet boy is better tonight. I have Bessie and Harry Reitz again for music, and have also Muriel and Gerald Pilditch, Millie Lean, Bertha Michaelson and Grace Anderson, so am getting on. Bob is in the 'Wacht Kamer' until 12 o'clock tonight, that is better than tramping for five hours! But oh! thank goodness he is not at the front!! I am very sleepy, so will close here.

The outbreak of war caused particular problems in the Cape Colony, where feelings among the white population were mixed and loyalties often very uncertain. While there was a large and vociferous English-speaking section who fully supported the war and many of the Dutch- or Afrikaans-speaking people were loyal to the Crown, the allegiance of others was dubious.

A few days before the war began, the Prime Minister, W.P. Schreiner, sent a telegram to all Resident Magistrates and Field Cornets to request their support in keeping the peace and preventing outbreaks of 'racial antagonism' ('rassentegenstreving'), and the reaction of D.J. Viljoen of Stuurmansrivier may be quoted as typical of many. In spite of the assurances of general loyalty, however, the resentment expressed by Viljoen at the presence of British troops massing on the borders of the Orange Free State and the feelings of solidarity with 'our brethren in the Republics' were both ominous. [Translation on p. 150.]

Stuurmans Rivier, 11 Oct. 1899

Den Edele Heer Schreiner, Premier

Mijnheer, – UEdls. telegram ontvangen. Ik ben zeer verblijd dat ik reeds in dien geest werkzaam was. De gemoederen zijn zeer opgewonnen, maar tot hier toe heb ik nog niemand ontmoet die men kan beschuldigen van dislojaliteit.

Men zijn alleen gehecht aan de Kroon, maar men verfoeidt het Kapitalisten Kliek wiens poletiek thans door het Imperiale Gouvernement uitgevoerd worden.

Wij betreuren het ten zeerste dat Imperiale troepen hier tusschen ons geplaats worden, en die dan scheint te meenen dat zij op private eigendomen kunnen doen wat zij willen.

Mijnheer, wij zijn *lojaal*, maar geloof mij onze harten bloedt en onze oogen weent over onze broederen in de Republieken die in een onrechtvaardig oorlog gesleept worden.

Ik verblijf, Mijnheer, UEdls. onderdanige dienaar, D.J. Viljoen.

'Ik zal mijn best doen,' wired Field Cornet Mostert from Oudtshoorn in his reply to Schreiner.

Once the war had begun, the Boer Republics made no immediate effort to harness the actual or latent sympathy among the Dutch-speaking inhabitants of the Cape Colony. It was not until 13 November that the invasion of the northern Cape was under-taken: Aliwal North, Colesberg, Burgersdorp, Barkly East and other towns in the area were occupied, and by the end of November, Chief Commandant J.H. Olivier of the Free State was approaching Dordrecht in the north-eastern Cape with his commando. During this period J.W. Sauer, Commissioner of Public Lands in the Schreiner cabinet, undertook a tour of the northern districts of the colony in order to appeal to the inhabitants to remain loyal to the Crown and not support the invaders. On 27 November he addressed a public meeting at Dordrecht, as telegraphed to Schreiner by the

17

Resident Magistrate of the Wodehouse Division, Frederick Whitham.

27.11.99

Premier, Rondebosch. – Two seventh November. Large meeting this morning. About five hundred present. Mr Sauer spoke most impressively at length and with great effect, impressing loyalty, necessity of abstaining from participation, and urgent strong expression of intention to have nothing to do with inroad of enemy's forces. The following Resolution was carried without a single dissentient, viz. – This meeting [of] Afrikanders residing Wodehouse Division deplores existing war, and expresses earnest intention not to take part in it.

Resolved to send delegates at once to Free State Commando [*sic*] with earnest protestation staying invasion by his forces this District, and to hand him a copy of this Resolution. The delegates appointed are: Dominus [=*Dominee*] Marais, de Wet, Member, Marais, a farmer, and Vermooten, an attorney. They are leaving at once, and expect to meet Commando somewhere this side Barkly East. Expect result Wednesday. Satisfactory so far, and people will stick to Resolution.

Schreiner's somewhat guarded reply, as noted by him in the margin of the telegram, read, 'Earnestly hope resolution may have result of saving district from invasion. Your energy and devotion are appreciated by me, even though I can not always agree with your views.' His doubts were, in the event, not misplaced, for the delegates sent to protest against the invasion in fact established amicable relations with the invaders. This unforeseen development did Sauer's reputation much harm with the pro-war party, and further discredited the Schreiner Cabinet.

Dordrecht was duly occupied and annexed by the Free Staters, but they moved no further into the Colony. On the same day on which the above message was despatched to Schreiner in Cape Town, a telegram was sent by President Steyn ordering Olivier to fall back and concentrate his forces on Stormberg, Naauwpoort and Kimberley.

As Prime Minister, Schreiner was in a difficult position, and his attempts to preserve the neutrality of the Cape Colony grew increasingly desperate as the feelings aroused by the war became more extreme on both sides.

A relatively minor issue which soon raised its head here as elsewhere in that racially sensitive society was the use of non-whites in combat, and however liberal Schreiner may have been in the context of nineteenth-century South Africa, he clearly agreed that the conflict should remain what was in the language of the day known as a 'white man's war'. The following exchange of telegrams took place between J.J. Graham, Secretary of the Law Department in Cape Town, and Lt. Col. Davies at Sterkstroom in the Stormberg region, presumably after complaints had been lodged or questions raised about an incident involving 'native privates'.

18

6. 'The Hon. W.P. Schreiner, Prime Minister of Cape Colony, 1898-1900', a studio portrait by Elliott & Fry. (From, The Times History of the War in South Africa, IV)

Telegram, 1.1.1900. Secretary Law Department, Cape Town. [To] Lieutenant Colonel Davies, Sterkstroom. No 3. First. Your No. 10. In what capacity were the native privates engaged?

– 1.1.1900. No 15. Your No. 3. Native privates were employed as part of relief patrol under Capt. Halse. Shall be glad of early authority as asked to replace saddlery, horses being procured.

– 2.1.1900. No. 11. Second. Your number fifteen of first. The point is, were the native privates engaged in combatant capacity? Were they armed? If so, how?

– 2.1.1900. No. 17. Your No. 11. The native private in question being a Bastard

7. 'Stamping out the rebellion in the Aliwal North district – rebels surrendering their arms at the Court House, Lady Grey', a photograph taken by F.W. Church after the first Free State invasion of the Cape Colony in the early stages of the war. (Cape Times Weekly, 23.5.1900)

was allowed in the fighting line. He was armed with a M[artini] H[enry]. The rest of the natives were utilized for holding horses under cover.

– *3.1.1900.* [*Further telegram from Davies.*] No. 3. Your No. 45. Major Naylan, with Captains Schenk and Rayner, four lieutenants, one hundred and forty-six Europeans and eighty-six natives, all C.P. We are holding position at Molteno, a severe engagement is still proceeding there, the enemy shelling heavily. Stop. At one time he was said to be surrounded, but has beaten off the Boers, and rein-forcements have been sent him.

– *68. Fourth. Your No. 17 of 2nd.* You have not fully answered my No. 11 of 2nd. Were the native privates engaged on the relief patrol armed? If so, how were they armed? These questions apply to all natives, whether employed holding horses under cover or otherwise, as it is a matter of first importance that natives should not be engaged as combatants, and the rule must be regarded as extending to Bastards.

– *4.1.00.* No 10, your 68. Speaking generally our natives are armed only with revolvers. In the case of those however under notice, Martini rifles were issued to them by the General upon Captain Halse's representations. Have already informed latter officer that such rifles must be returned to store, and intend seeing the General on his return on the subject.

In the original, 'eighty-six natives' has been underlined by Schreiner and annotated, 'Urged strongly on H.E. that native police should not be brought into action in this war, W.P.S., 4.1.00'; the reference is to 'His Excellency', the Governor, Sir Alfred Milner. This was to remain the general endeavour of the white combatants, although the principle lost some of its force as the war went on. 'I must say I do not like this employment of natives,' wrote Captain B.J. Jones of the 1st Leinster Regiment in the north-eastern Free State towards the end of 1901 after having sent out four armed scouts (by implication blacks) to reconnoitre. 'It is not that I see anything wrong in using native troops against a white enemy; I hold it justifiable to employ soldiers of any colour provided you take care their behaviour is that of civilised men, but once a pledge however foolish is given it should be kept.'

To return to Schreiner: in the difficult circumstances in which he found himself during the first months of the war, it cannot have been much consolation to him to receive the following letter from The Picture Postcard Co. Ltd, London.

The Hon W.P. Schreiner, Cape Town.

Sir, – We take the liberty of sending you herewith a series of post-cards containing portraits of the prominent men on the British and Boer side in connection with the present war, amongst which you will find your own and several of your friends' which have just been issued by this Company and of which we beg your kind acceptance.

We are, Sir, yours obediently, The Picture Postcard Co. Ltd, J.V. Hopefield, Secretary.

'Ackd. with thanks, 9/1/00', runs the annotation on this missive.

How deeply divisive the war could be in South African society, even in its early stages, is demonstrated in the ranks of Schreiner's own family. His wife was a sister of the Transvaal Secretary of State, F.W. Reitz, while his own sister, the novelist and polemicist Olive Schreiner, was a prominent supporter of the Boers, as was her husband, S.C. Cronwright-Schreiner; another sister, Henrietta Stakesby Lewis, and a brother, Theo Schreiner, were active in expressing their loyalty to the British Empire and their support of the British cause.

Mrs Stakesby Lewis (Ettie or Het Schreiner) was a social and temperance worker and preacher of remarkable energy and talents, who in her day was as well known in South Africa as any other member of the family. Her statements on the war are not in theselves remarkable, apart from their eloquence and vigour; they deserve attention, however, because her opposition to the Boers seems to have been based mainly on their treatment of what she described in her 'Prayer of Peace' as 'The helpless native peoples of this land': 'she thought the Boer did not treat the Native properly,' as Cronwright-Schreiner succinctly

8. *The Pretoria Commando, 1899, a photograph from the collections of the South African Library on which no further information is given.*

put it. There were not many white people in South Africa or beyond to whom this was a factor of great importance at the time.

The following letter to W.P. Schreiner from his sister refers to a statement on the war which she had sent to the Methodist Times in England under the title 'A Voice from South Africa', and which was subsequently also published as a pamphlet entitled A Message from South Africa to the Christian people of Great Britain, by Mrs Lewis, sister of the Prime Minister of Cape Colony. She wrote from 'The Highlands' in Vredehoek, Cape Town, where she ran a home for alcoholics. Her remark on Schreiner taking office 'when and how you did' probably refers to the fact that he had come to power with the support of the Afrikaner Bond, which would have been abhorrent to her.

The Highlands, Jan. 28th, 1900

Dear old Will, – I send herewith a paper with an article in it which I felt it *my duty* to write at this juncture to the Christian World of England.

I want you to know that I am *not responsible* for the placing of my name as it

9. *The arrival at the Cape Town Docks of the* Dunnotar Castle *on 10 January 1900, with Lord Roberts, appointed to supreme command of the British Army in South Africa after the debacles of the previous year, and his chief-of-staff, Major-General Lord Kitchener. Khaki uniforms, military helmets and top hats on the quayside, and a throng of interested passengers on deck.* (PHA)

appears in the forefront of that article. I purposely headed it simply 'A Voice from South Africa: a message to, &c.', because I felt that if it was God's message it needed and should have no human interest attaching to it. I did not say one word about my relationship to you, simply *signed* my name as I do *all* important letters or papers, H.R.S. Lewis née Schreiner. I am grieved, because I feel sure you would rather our relationship was not referred to in connection with such an article, but you will understand that I cannot help it, and I am sure you will know it is not a sort of thing I would do or countenance.

As to the article itself, of course you may not at all agree with it, but you will know that when I believe with my whole soul that the truth concerning this war is as I have there stated it, I could not keep silence when I know a number of fellow Christians are not realizing or knowing what I believe to be a truth they should know, that they may act *aright* at this time.

It's hard, bitter hard, dear old Will, to have to take steps you will be so opposed to, for I love you, as you know, you and yours, as I love few things on earth, but the *call of duty* is to me as clear to let my voice be heard on this matter at this crisis as it was to you to take office when and how you did.

I only pray that as truly as you have fulfilled a glorious mission for the country, though at terrible cost, by obeying 'the call of duty' as it came to you, so may my effort to follow the call laid on me bring some blessing to the cause of truth and justice. I should like you to know that I have never failed to bless God for the beauty of your faithful life-following of duty, and have in the tremendous trials through which your dear life has been passing borne it up ceaselessly in faith and prayer, asking strength and wisdom and comfort for you.

In the *agony* of the present conflict it has been an unspeakable comfort to me to see in your life and its brave fulfilment of its high mission cause to praise God and bless His grace in you. And however what I have written, and still shall have to write and speak, may cause you to feel towards me, I would like you to know that while I live I shall always be in my intense personal devotion to you, your old Het.

In his affectionate reply dated 29 January, on writing paper headed 'Prime Minister's Office', Schreiner remarked rather obscurely, 'For my part I am quite certain that in what you have done you have acted honestly but in the dark – where it seems fit that the sons and daughters of men should dwell in these days in all humility and quiet endurance. Other eyes and other days may see the light beyond these clouds, but neither you nor I shall live outside the glories that this triumph of evil as we can know it has spread about us like a pall.' It must be borne in mind that the Schreiners were the children of a missionary, and all, in their very different ways, deeply religious, as well as rather odd.

The violence of the opposition and the vituperation which Schreiner encountered is shown in many of the letters preserved among his papers, among which are several sent anonymously, such as the following one from Australia. It was accompanied by clippings from the Melbourne Age *criticising his conduct in the war, one of which was headed 'The traitor Schreiner'.*

Hobart, Tasmania, March 26, 1900

Your miserable Traitor, – Before this reaches you I sincerely trust you may have received what you so richly deserve, that is a *'traitor's death'*. Shooting is far too good for such a *'traitorous reptile'* as you have proved yourself to be. Far rather would I be the Traitor Guener[?] than the so named Premier Schreiner. When you come to the end of your tether, may the spirits of those soldiers who you have been the cause of their death rise up and curse you.

Wishing you all the punishments of a Traitor. Yours, A Tasmanian.

The Hon. W.P. Schreiner, Premier and 'Traitor' of The Cape.

10. 'Government House party': the High Commissioner and Governor of the Cape Colony, Sir Alfred Milner (centre), with a group which includes his private secretary, Osmond Walrond (standing on the right). (Cape Times Weekly, 14.7.1897)

After Bloemfontein had been occupied by the British in March 1900, 20 000 people thronged Greenmarket Square in Cape Town to support the proposed annexation of the Boer Republics, and a large number marched to Government House to cheer the Governor, Sir Alfred Milner. On their way they encountered Schreiner on the corner of Adderley and Wale Streets, returning from lunch, and he was mobbed amid 'tremendous hooting and hissing' by what a newspaper described as a crowd of 'gigantic proportions', from which he had to be rescued by the police.

This incident, revealing as it is of Schreiner's unpopularity at the time, called forth the following personal note from Milner's secretary, Osmond Walrond of Harrow and Balliol, who cannot be presumed to have sympathised with Schreiner's views, but whose sense of fair play was obviously outraged by the excesses of the lower classes.

Private

Government House, Cape Town, 4.4.00

Dear Mr Schreiner, – I just write a line to tell you how I am disgusted at those beastly shopkeeper fellows for what I read happened yesterday. I am sorry I was not there with you or would have given then a piece of my mind. Yours sincerely, Osmond Walrond.

As the pro-war party in the Cape Colony grew more vocal and more militant, Schreiner's position became untenable, however, and after an irreparable split in his Cabinet he resigned on 13 June 1900.

11. (opposite). '5.30 a.m. on the Market Square during the siege of Kimberley, waiting for meat ration'; a photograph by F.H. Hancox (detail). (INIL 597)

THE SIEGES
(1899-1902)

While a number of smaller towns were captured by Boer forces invading Natal and the Cape Colony during the first weeks of the war, a few large towns held out and underwent a protracted period of siege, most notably Ladysmith, Kimberley and Mafeking.

Among the day-to-day records of the long siege of Ladysmith is that of M.W. Tyler, conductor of the Supply and Transport Corps attached to the 24th British Field Hospital in the town. His diary consists of three small black notebooks recording his experiences in the war from September 1899 to February 1902, the first of them inscribed 'For my dear wife'.

The extract given below covers a period of heavy shelling and repeated Boer attacks during the first weeks of the siege. 'Tin Town' or the 'Tin Camp' was the Ladysmith barracks on the outskirts of the town, which was abandoned at an early stage because of its proximity to the Boer lines; Sir George White was the officer commanding the Natal Field Force, who had allowed himself to be shut up in the beleaguered town.

8th Nov. '99. Another gun found voice today and dropped shells in the Tin Camp, which had been vacated. Boers can be seen in different positions. All tents have been struck and ambulances brought under cover. The gunners are working in shirtsleeves like slaves. The guns have kept up a continual roar.

8 a.m. One sailor just brought in with a shell wound on his right shoulder. The Medical Officer fears that it must be amputated.

10 a.m. Quite a change. The infantry are engaged all round Ladysmith. The fighting today has been severe, last[ing?] altogether 15 hours, but at last the enemy have been forced to retire. The result of course can never be known.

9.11.99. 5 a.m. Firing commenced by the enemy shelling the 5th Lancers and 19th Hussars, who were moving out to their bivouac. Although several shells [were] sent right amongst them, none was hit. The infantry are again at it, and many shells are falling uncomfortably near us.

3.30 p.m. Removed one officer and four men wounded to Town Hall hospital.

This has been the most terrible day I have ever experienced, what with shells screaming and bursting all round us (over 20 into our Hospital) it seems a miracle that we are alive to tell the tale. One shell passed over my head and burst 20 yards in rear of me.

12. The ordinariness of war: 'Guards' field pay office (Ladysmith garrison),' runs the original caption, and continues: 'Guard of Gordon Highlanders removing on account of shelling. This guard also furnished sentries for the Standard Bank opposite, which was abandoned owing to the building being repeatedly struck by shells.' Amidst death and destruction, the camera of Henry Kisch records only the wide, empty street and desultory traffic of a colonial town. (From, The Siege of Ladysmith in 120 Pictures)

10.11.99. Everybody was up early and the tents cleared, breakfast eaten and all cleared to cover. The day, however, passed over without much excitement. Rumours state that the Boers have cleared. Hot!

11.11.99. Shelling again commenced at 10 a.m., several bursting in town, Barrett and myself having two very close to us. No damage was done, and everything was quiet by 11 p.m.

Some of the men on the positions say they saw Boers removing their dead in buck wagons to different farms. Our loss in two days was eighteen killed and wounded. The Boer loss is estimated at 700(?).

12.11.99, Sunday. The Boers do not fight to-day, being at prayers(?). It is generally believed that the prayers consist of mounting guns in different positions. Some of the Boers sent in yesterday for food. (Not necessary.) Medical assistance.[1] Sir G.

1. Punctuation as in the original.

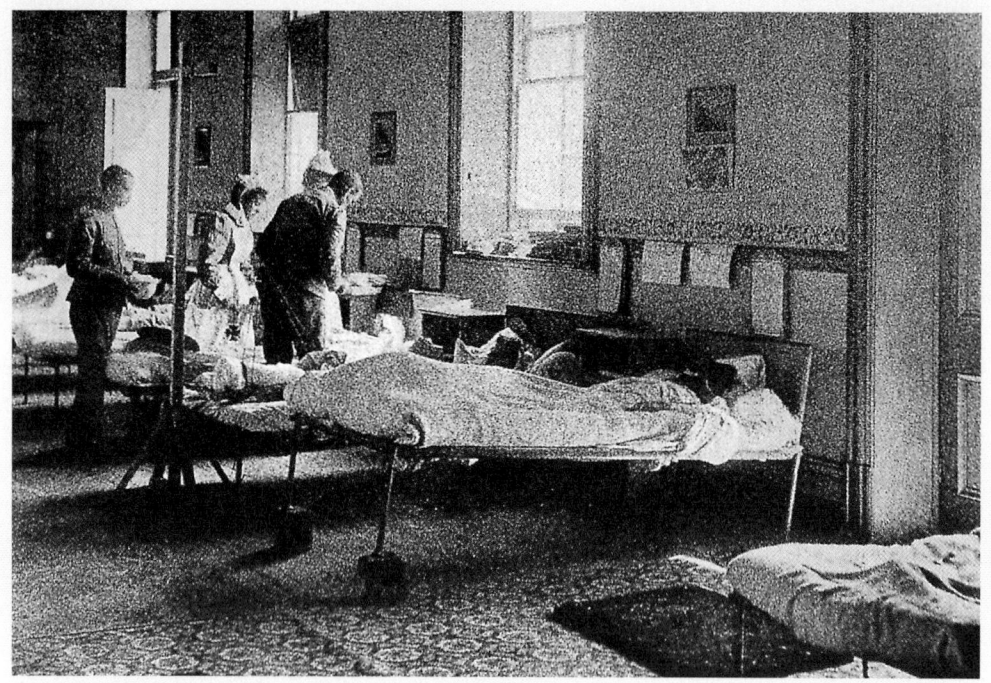

13. 'Hospital ward in Town Hall: closed owing to the danger from falling shells, one of which passed through the ward, killing one man and wounding others.' Another photograph from the besieged Ladysmith by Henry Kisch, showing patterned linoleum, stencilled dadoes and nurses in starched aprons, cuffs and caps in the summer heat of Natal. (From, The Siege of Ladysmith in 120 Pictures)

White is said to have told them that he would send what medical comforts he could spare and what medical assistance is considered necessary, but food could not be supplied at any cost.

All our troops are cheerful, but although a river (Klip River) is running through Ladysmith, no one is allowed to wash.

13.11.99. 5 a.m. Again the morning broke with the roar of artillery and kept up with varying fierceness till 1 p.m. without any further damage than smashing an ambulance wagon and killing some mules.

14.11.99. Firing again broke the day and the usual cannonade of artillery was indulged in. At 11 a.m. we sent out three batteries covered by cavalry to the south west of the camp, and they shelled all the ridges round, killing a number of Boers. Guns opened on the troops from five different positions, but only one of our artillery was wounded in the arm. He was immediately dressed and removed to the Town Hall.

In the town one man of the BMR's had his head shot away by a shell whilst asleep in his bivouac. The Royal Hotel was damaged, and a house used as an Officers' Mess was hit, but the damage in both cases was slight.

J.B. Jardine, who has already been encountered at Pietermaritzburg shortly before the outbreak of war (pp. 10-12 above), succeeded in catching up with his Regiment and being 'on the spot'. He too found himself in Ladysmith during the siege, and the following notes describe Christmas in the town. By this time the siege had been going on for almost two weeks, but champagne was still obtainable if one had the right contacts. Sir Redvers Buller was in command of the Natal Field Force, and Intombi was a neutral camp for sick, wounded and non-combatants outside the town.

22nd December 1899. At Stables this morning a shell from the big gun on Telegraph Hill (a ricochet) did a good deal of damage. Fawcett, King, Wathen, Oakes and Hulse were wounded, more or less slightly. Four horses had to be shot and three others were wounded. Sergeant-Major Harris had his right eye damaged and will probably lose his sight in it. Fawcett lost the middle finger of his right hand and was wounded in both legs.

On the 15th Buller lost a thousand killed and wounded, and he says the Boers lost 600: he also lost ten guns, which had rashly got within 300 yards of the Boer rifle fire.

The shelling was frequent all day.

24th December 1899, Sunday. Fawcett and Hooper have gone to Intombi Camp; the latter is supposed to have typhoid. To-day there was no shelling, except one or two in the early dawn.

25th December 1899, Christmas Day. The Boers did not shell as much, knowing, I suppose, that I considered it a holiday. The weather is still very hot and we all long for rain, especially as horses and cattle are suffering from want of grass. The first case of horse sickness occurred this morning.

Cannot call this exactly a 'Merry Christmas'. Wondered what one's people were saying and doing very many times during the day. Here we are only one and a half hours ahead of British time; in India there was a much greater difference. Drank absent friends in champagne we were lucky to get from the Leicesters.

The sick in the Regiment are increasing day by day and typhoid is going strong. If Buller does not join up with us soon, that disease and horse sickness will cripple the Regiment. Short rations are weakening the horses more and more every day: I don't think they can go very far even now.

26th December 1899, Tuesday. The Boers have discovered Sir George White's new residence, and gave it three shells this morning in sucession. They were good shots, but did not actually strike the house. Hulse is still very seedy with fever; I hope it is not enteric.

Dixon, 16th Lancers, went out with a flag of truce a few days ago, when a Boer asked him if his friends were not getting rather sick of all this, as they themselves were. Dixon said 'No; if we were not soldiering here, we should have to be somewhere else, so that it did not matter really.'

The two accounts of the siege of Ladysmith quoted above are by men directly exposed to and involved in the fighting. The two descriptions of life in the besieged Kimberley which follow are by women, who inevitably occupied the position of onlookers in what was very much a war conducted by men, and therefore provide a somewhat different perspective on the events.

The first of these texts is taken from a long diary letter to 'My own darling Mother and all' begun at Woodley Street, Kimberley, on 20 October 1899, and completed after the relief of the town the following February. The author was an Englishwoman named Elizabeth Atkinson, who is believed to have been a schoolteacher; all that is known of her for certain is that she died before 1926, when her husband, by that time living in England again, had her diary published privately under the title Personal Experiences and Recollections of the Siege of Kimberley, by my dear wife Elizabeth Atkinson. *In the foreword it is described as 'the simple narrative of one of the many varied experiences in a life crowded in very full measure in incident, in which she ever took a foremost part!'*

Before the advent of photocopying, the South African Library often obtained rare or obscure published items in the form of typed transcriptions which were catalogued as manuscripts. It is in this form that the diary of Elizabeth Atkinson was obtained by the Library, and it still forms part of the manuscript collections, even though a copy of the printed text was acquired many years later. It is an attractive little book, and the Library's copy bears an inscription from Willie Atkinson to 'Dear Agnes and Fred', to whom it was presented 'as a reminder of the very beautiful life of our darling Lizzie'. Strictly speaking, the diary of Elizabeth Atkinson cannot be considered as an unpublished manuscript for the purposes of this book. However, as it is a lively and vivid account of the siege, and as the published text is not generally known or widely available, two extracts have been included here on the strength of the typescript copy in the manuscript collection.

Martial law had been proclaimed in Kimberley on 15 October, the 'last Sunday' referred to at the beginning of Mrs Atkinson's letter. 'Willie' was her husband, who seems to have been away from home when the war began and to have got back to Kimberley only just in time.

Before war was declared I was one of the many who thought that, though every preparation was being made, actual warfare would not commence. As I knew you could do no good, and perhaps did not know much about it, and also as it was almost impossible to write without dilating on the situation, I refrained from writing altogether.[1] Now we are besieged by the Boers; and though no one thinks they will take K[imberley], yet there is enough danger for us all to feel that we are really amidst the sound of war's alarm. And we have really had war's alarm.

1. Footnote in the original, 'October 15th, when we were first cut off.' This refers to the suspension of railway communications from Kimberley to the south.

14. An unidentified young soldier from the album of the Jeffreys family; a commercial studio photograph by Treadway of Ladysmith. (Jeffreys Album)

Last Sunday morning the war signal – a fearful hooter used in the Kimberley mine – sounded in church, and after the prayer all the men left the church. We stayed awhile but were manifestly uneasy, and eventually the service was brought to an abrupt conclusion, and we were in the streets and going to the nearest quarter for news. This was very conflicting, and you would be astonished now if you could have seen the place to which we wended our way: the Gardens, the gates of which Agnes made several copies, are now occupied by the Imperial and Volunteer troops, tents rest in every direction, and patrols are stationed at every point. Martial law is proclaimed, and all have to be in their houses at nine o'clock, unless they wish to be arrested as spies.

To our immediate news. Willie had to run the gauntlet in getting home in safety, leaving by the last coach and last train, and when finally reaching British territory

15. Elizabeth Atkinson, a portrait from the published version of her account of the siege.

was led by two English armed police before the Chief guarding the Border to be questioned as to name and race, etc., so that they would be assured he was no Dutch spy. This delayed so much that he and his companions had to remain at Fourteen Stream station, which was occupied by 175 armed British police who were nightly expecting an attack from the Boers. He was thankful to have reached home on Sunday, for on the Monday martial law was proclaimed, and it is problematical whether he would have got here till after the siege was raised. Imagine then what our anxiety would have been.

The reason he left it so late was that he did not wish to give up his billet, as he is sick of so many changes. However, he had no alternative, and of course after the war is over everything will be in a better condition for Britishers.

We hear that Mafeking is giving a good account of itself and holding its own under Baden-Powell. But doubtless you will have heard all our news before we have who are in siege. I expect now you are having your fears relieved, for though you know we are besieged, you will know there has been no attack, only looting (stealing) round about, and the Waterworks pumps blown up. We have water supply for a month, but we are compelled to be careful, and it is only running two hours a day.

Willie was working at the engines now blown up when you were with me. What changes a few years do make, to be sure! Who then would have thought there would be war; but it really began the Christmas after you left, in the 'Jameson Raid' of which you must have heard and read.

Elizabeth Atkinson's diary of the siege is complemented by an extensive but incomplete diary letter begun at Newton, Kimberley, on 14 October and addressed to 'My dear Sisters'. It was found among the papers of Sophia Hendriksz, whose family lived in the Somerset West area and were related by marriage to the Cape politician J.H. Hofmeyr ('Onze Jan'), Chairman of the Afrikaner Bond. Among the papers of the Bond in the South African Library there is, somewhat unexpectedly, an exchange of telegrams dispatched during the siege concerning the whereabouts and welfare of Johanna Hendriksz, whose address was given as 'c/o Miss Immelman, Mission House, 13 Lawson Street'; it can probably be assumed that she was the author of this letter.

On 4 November, the day before the first entry reproduced below, Chief Commandant C.J. Wessels had demanded the surrender of the town. At the same time he expressed his willingness to receive in his camp 'any Africanders who are desirous of leaving Kimberley' should this be refused, an offer which was accepted by one family only. Johanna Hendriksz with her friends and relatives had freely elected to remain behind in the threatened town, but it is probable that they were nonetheless more favourably disposed to the Boer cause than the English-speaking community of Kimberley among whom they found themselves. Her account of the siege is therefore not merely that of a woman in a situation dominated by men, but to some extent also that of a non-British outsider who did not fully share the prevailing sentiments about the war.

Like most younger people who had received their education in the Cape Colony, Johanna Hendriksz wrote English more easily and naturally than Dutch, but she obviously spoke and thought in Afrikaans, e.g. 'I am enjoying myself yet' for 'still' (Afrikaans 'nog'), which sometimes gives an unintentionally comic effect to her diary entries.

Wessels' demand for surrender having been rejected, the bombardment of the town by the Boers began somewhat tentatively on 6 November, the anticipated 'awful day' of the second diary entry.

Sunday, 5 [November 1899]. A fine day, all well. I just commenced playing hymns when I heard an officer at the door with some soldiers coming to take away the rails with which our house is fenced in, I daresay to fence in the whole place, because they are doing it at every house. I continued to play and sing, but the noise is so terrible I had to cease. I hope to go to church yet and receive a blessing. Fancy to wait for Sunday again to do the work, how grieved our Saviour must be.

I was in church, but when coming home found Sophy in tears and busy packing in, she got notice to clear in 24 hours, the house must be blown down, Aunt Lenie's and Annie's also. So you can imagine in what a state we were on the holy day. The people are all very kind though. Oom Philipie at once took all my clothes over and said I must stay with them and be their child, where they go I must go too. I thank the Lord for His goodness.

Monday, 6th [November]. Today is expected to be the awful day, at [*sic*] yet all is quiet, it is over nine o'clock and at twelve o'clock the shooting will commence. I feel quite safe under the wings of the Almighty.

We went to see Mrs Morkel's house, they have all left some weeks already, and tonight about twenty came to search the house. All the nice fruit trees are destroyed. Philip has found a nice place too, and so all the others.

It is four o'clock already and no alarm yet. All quiet, we have just returned from the market, where we packed in everything we could get hold of now they are busy bringing it away.

The house will also be destroyed, and none of the whole family here, except a friend of them who had to see to everything. It is more like Sunday today then [*sic*] yesterday.

7 o'clock. The alarm is on, so we cannot go to prayer meeting.

Tuesday, 7th [November]. This morning shells comes showering into the town, but as yet did no damage, they must be far off. I do not feel afraid, has been twice to Mrs Pienaar, who has moved near to the church and is sick. I am glad the Lord has shown me of what use I can be.

Wednesday, 8th [November]. I awoke to hear the loud shots of the shells, [I] counted five, then I jumped up, dressed and went to see what is going on. All was calm then, but the locusts are packed in the garden, awful things they are.

Poor Mrs Morkel's house are nearly quite gone, but Aunt Lenie and Sophy are not touched yet. I have not been to my patient this morning yet, will try to go just now. I do not feel so well either, my liver is troubling me so.

The afternoon we went to the Home, I [*sic*] heart felt so sad to see all the orphans, but they seemed to be nicely cared for. Cousin Letty called them together and made them [sing?], Jezus is a rock in a weary land, tears came into my eyes.

Thursday, 9th [November]. All well and quiet yet. I went to fetch Jannie to spend the day with us, he is so good. Annie['s] house is quite gone also, and Mr Morkel's too. I met Cousin Johanna, she asked me to call on her. I was not there for some time, as she said something that hurt me awfully. Now it is over.

Friday, 10th [November]. Quite calm, is [*sic*] if nothing is going on. I got up early,

36

as it gets so warm in the day. We went out calling, the people all complain about the food getting so scarce [*sic*], even the many horses will not have any forage within a short time. People are telling me that I will not be able to get away within five months. The Lord's will be done.

Saturday, 11th [November]. Quite early we heard a patroul passed our door, and not long after loud shelling on three sides was heard. We got up, and when outside could see from where the firing comes and where they burst. They are firing from three different forts here and two from the Boers' side. I think it will continue now. We also heard the rifle firing of the patroul, but have not heard the result yet.

While I write the shelling goes on. Mimmie is watching them yet. Under circumstances I am enjoying myself yet. I trust the Lord is comforting.

I heard yesterday all the houses are to be searched for arms and ammunition. They do wonderful things here. Sophy's house is still spared, I hope they will not touch it.

It is rather cold this morning after the intense heat. At present it is quiet. Half past nine, it seems to [*sic*] fight is over for today. The patroul has come back with their waggon of wounded. Before they came we saw two riderless horses come running on. Now I know what war means.

The shellings has commenced again, I stood looking from where they comes and where they fell. I hear it did some damages [in] a few places.

It was not until February 1900 that Kimberley was relieved as part of a general British advance, and Elizabeth Atkinson described the final weeks of the siege in her letter home, which was completed only after it had ended. Amidst the disruption and dislocation of war, Mrs Atkinson's gratitude for the patronising kindness of 'our Mayor Mr Oliver' to 'Willie and I', her appreciation of the 'beaming smile and salute' of Cecil Rhodes, and her chagrin at not being introduced to him, Mr Oliver being 'always in a hurry', sound a note of English suburban snobbery closer to The Diary of a Nobody *than to death and destruction on the veld.*

Col. R.G. Kekewich was the officer responsible for the defence of the town.

Of course, the sickness increased as time went on, and we all had our times of general seediness, But I think the mothers of families with little babies suffered by far the most, especially if they had not ready cash; milk was so hard to get, and after the hanging about for hours sometimes so small in quantity. It was just the same in getting – or trying to get – meat. I have felt so sorry as I have passed lines of Kaffirs packed closely up one behind the other at the back of the two places where meat could be obtained. The white people were often very crowded trying to get their meat the first. The folk spent hours and hours daily trying to get food to last for the two days. I shudder to think what would have been the case if martial law had not been proclaimed and foodstuffs with prices apportioned out. We have a lot

16. 'Siege of Kimberley: bomb proof shelters for families in Kenilworth.' (INIL 12453)

to be thankful for to Col. Kekewich and the military authorities. I hear he is to the recipient of a 'Sword of Honour' from the people of K[imberley], and it will have been well earned.

Now I must attempt to describe the flying to places of refuge upon the advent of the dreaded 100-pounders. Marvellous escapes have been experienced during the whole siege, but never in such numbers as in the last week. We suffered the heavy bombardment from Wednesday, February 7th, to Sunday morning, before a great number of the people had any shelter. Meanwhile redoubts in central places were being rapidly constructed, and on Sunday soldiers on horseback went from house to house telling all that they go from four o'clock in the afternoon and take shelter down the two big mines and various redoubts. Provisions would be supplied, but they were to take as much as possible for the first few hours, to provide themselves with blankets and pillows, and not to over-load themselves.

Sunday was quiet from the Boers' shells, but what a dreadful time some of those poor people passed before they got snug in the mine, and always with the fear that at twelve o'clock, midnight, the shelling would begin. However, that did not happen, and though all that could be [was] done to alleviate the dreadful waiting time on the top, individual cases of extreme suffering were endured, the recital of which causes the more fortunate people who were not obliged to go down for safety to

17. *'Scenes in Kimberley during the siege: a bomb-proof trench where people sheltered during the bombardment.' A newspaper photograph of the time which is unusual in showing a coloured family; note particularly the woman in the sun-bonnet in the entrance to the shelter.* (Cape Times Weekly, 7.3.1900)

creep with horror. Some after waiting were so ill when they got down that they had to come up again, preferring to brave the shells.

Of course there were many invalids, many weak, babies and old people; and imagine what the packing of these people meant down the long tunnels and galleries of the mine. I believe there were 1400 people packed in the De Beers Mine also, and an equally great crowd in the Kimberley. Can you imagine the scene, for it is impossible to describe it? The people lining these tunnels, with little children, bundles and no – or very little – light. There was no panic, with all the discomfort or crowd [sic] and the long waits, but many returned to their homes again. Our friends the Scotts waited till nearly midnight, and seemed as far off as ever getting into the mines, so returned to face the shelling. Fortunately, though many passed near and over their and our house, none actually struck the premises; only in Scott's back garden a large splinter was picked up. The roofs of the whole block had debris cast upon them, and in Park's buildings, which, you remember, adjoins our right-hand, there were splinters from shells through the roof and in the house.

Personally I was safely housed at the residence of our Mayor. Mr Oliver overtook Willie and I as we were hastening out of the line of fire, several [shells] passing

18. *The ordinariness of war: 'Kimberley mounted troops returning from engagement with the Boers, Nov. 25th 1899, Transvaal Horse', photographed by Bennett. A brick wall, corrugated iron, a wide, dusty pavement, sparsely shaded, a few spectators, both black and white, and somewhere to one side a group of mounted soldiers passing by in the heat of the day.* (INIL 12470)

directly over our house, on Thursday one bursting so near the front that we could see the smoke and dust as it fell to the ground and smell the horrid fumes. When Mrs Oliver asked me to stay we were very glad, as Willie's redoubt was right opposite, and of course at such times one was very anxious to see one's nearest as often as possible. He used to come over sometimes twice and always once a day.

Mrs Oliver's baby girl was three weeks old only, and as both the cook and nurse left to go down the mines for safety with their relatives, I was able to look after Muriel, Elsie and Edgar, and see that they were in the shell-proof when the shells whizzed over their house too. Janie Alexander, who had been staying at the Olivers', slept with me, and it was as pleasant as it could be in siege time. Janie did the cooking, Nurse looked after Mrs Oliver and baby, who were wonderfully well, and I generally helped in all three departments.

(. . .)

At the Olivers' I came more into touch with things at Headquarters than here. Mr Cecil Rhodes often came on business, and I had his beaming smile and salute more than once, though I did not get introduced; Mr O. was always in a hurry, and

40

19. 'Troops entering Ladysmith', the scene after the relief of the besieged town on 28 February 1900, with a military band (left foreground), some horses, and a sea of khaki uniforms in the heat and the dust of summer. (INIL 1407)

I suppose Mr Rhodes thought, as I stood on the verandah as he passed, that I was Mrs Oliver, who had not met him.

There was one very important meeting held at the Olivers' to blind the Boer spies, and at this meeting a strongly-worded message was sent to Lord Methuen urging our relief, and especially so on account of the heavy shells.

For some days after, in his odd moments, Mr O. was busy preparing his speech to Lord Methuen or Lord Roberts, whoever came to our relief. He read it me and it was very good.

On the Thursday afternoon I heard Mr O. call out to Janie as we were having a rest in the bedroom – it was very hot weather – 'Janie, the Relief Column is coming in.' He had previously arranged to drive her out in that direction, expecting relief may come at any hour. You cannot imagine our feelings! We jumped up, and in a little while she and Mr Oliver were off and we waited excitedly at home.

By and bye Willie came in, but later than usual, and he had actually viewed the Advance Column coming in and did not know it. All was excitement, and Muriel and I went over to his camp to see if we could have a view of their coming to their

41

encampment directly in front, but a mile away on the veldt, of Willie's fort. When we returned, not quite sure we had seen any of the troops of the Column – though we had – I found Janie all trembling with excitement and almost hysterical, for she had been the only lady with the Mayor when he stopped at the Half-way House (a canteen and the stables for [the] tram) and welcomed General French and his Staff. These went on to the Club, and I believe the ovation and screaming and shouting as the General made his way there beggars description.

If I had been at home I should have heard and seen him or the crowd, but Willie and I going to the Camp, we got too far from Dutoitspan Road to hear the shouts.

So we were actually relieved by little General French, who gained – or helped to do so – Elangslaagte [sic]. This redoubtable man was off with his troops to Dronfield, the scene of our first battle, where a terrible fight ensued and nearly 500 Boers were killed.

The Lancer who first spoke to Mr Oliver said, 'And where in the 6-inch gun?' It was a great disappointment to all when this hundred-pounder was successfully taken away by the Boers, and as nearly 800 of our own Kimberley troops went out about five o'clock to try to prevent them, rather a mystery to some of us. But I daresay as their system of intelligence is agreed by all to be wonderfully good (Dutch and other spies abounded in Kimberley), they knew in time to be out of reach before darkness fell, and then useless to try.

It was getting dark when General French entered the Club, and the scene of excitement and uproar was intensely interesting to those who were fortunate enough to be there. I heard General French was carried upon men's shoulders into the Club.

But things sobered now quickly enough, and we were quiet enough till the departure of the first train out of Kimberley and the arrival of the mail on the Thursday following – one week later.

20. (opposite). Green Point Common, Cape Town, where there was a British military camp during the early stages on the war, and later a camp for Boer prisoners of war; photograph by G.A.Walton, Johannesburg (detail). (PHA)

THE BRITISH
ADVANCE
(EARLY 1900)

*P*reparing *for what was already regarded as inevitable war in South Africa, the British military command decided in June 1899 that 'the main line of advance against the Transvaal should be based on the Cape Colony, and should follow generally the line of railway through the Orange Free State to Johannesburg and Pretoria'. Towards the end of November, in pursuance of this plan, the first infantry division under Lord Methuen began their advance along the railway line from the Orange River to the besieged Kimberley, the progress of the British forces being marked by the battles of Belmont, Enslin or Graspan, Modder River and Magersfontein.*

It is this phase of the war which is covered by the following extract from the diary of H.R. Langmore, civil surgeon with a British military hospital, who arrived at the Cape at the end of November and was ordered up to the interior shortly afterwards. The diary, a small, hard-covered notebook with a clasp, records his movements in South Africa until he returned to England at the end of 1900. During the first few weeks he seems to have made brief notes in this each day and to have worked them up in slightly more detail later. Even the fuller entries are terse enough, but they provide a graphic account of the alternating horror and boredom behind the scenes during the great battles of the period.

On 18 December, when it had become clear that this would not be a quick or easy war, Lord Roberts was appointed Commander-in-Chief in South Africa with Lord Kitchener as Chief of Staff. He reached Modder River on 8 February (a date left blank by Langmore in his diary), after which the tide began to turn in favour of the British.

On the December 6th [1899] four of the civil surgeons including myself received orders to proceed to Orange River, which was the advance base. Left Cape Town at 9 p.m., and after 43 hours' journey reached Orange River.

The first day we had a terrific thunderstorm and heavy rain which washed out the tents in which the sick and wounded were. There were a good many Boer wounded here. It was a great business getting the patients into comparatively dry tents. Next day we moved further from the railway station and back from the river to a higher piece of ground. I was now attached [to] Major Knapp's[?] hospital, together with Connacher, another civil surgeon.

Here we had plenty of work, and on the 12th received the wounded from

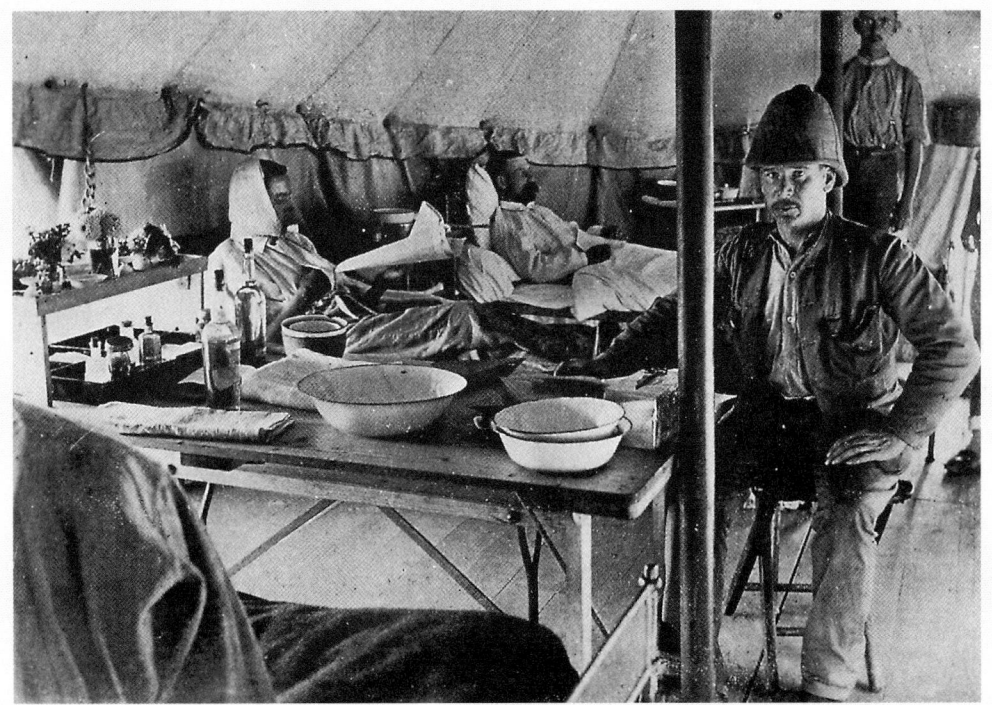

21. 'Inside a tent of No.2 General Hospital', by the Cape Town photographer Alf Hosking. (Cape Argus Weekly, 30.5.1900)

Magersfontein. Several train loads came down, and we were very busy. Dressing wounds from 11.30-6.30. The heat was great, flies a plague and dust storms of almost daily occurrence. Beyond a walk down to the Orange River (about 2 miles off) and a bathe there was little or nothing to do.

On Christmas Day dined with the Cape Field Hospital.

Connacher and I got leave to go to Modder River for the day. We went up early one morning and returned the evening of the next day. Were most hospitably put up by the Cape bearer company, who gave us horses and took us up to the ridge where the naval guns fired morning and evening at Magersfontein and over the Boer trenches at Modder River. Returned with two brass cases from the naval 15 lb. and a few cartridges, shells &c. from Modder River.

Shortly after, I saw the Surgeon-General at Orange River who had come up to inspect the hospitals, and asked to be sent up to Modder River. A few days after I received orders to go.

Here I joined the 1st Divisional Field Hospital (O.C. Major Coutts) and remained at Modder River about seven weeks. Our Mess consisted of the Major, Prof. Ogston[?], Capt. Lawson, Major Pallin A.V.D., myself and quartermaster. Was provided with a horse here and rode every morning at 6 a.m., the only time

22. 'Trenches at Magersfontein', a photograph by H. Eaton. The dramatic and unexpected British defeat at Magersfontein took place on 11 December 1899. (Cape Argus Weekly, 23.5.1900)

when it was at all cool – generally went up to the ridge. Fair bathing in the Modder. The Boers had blown up the railway bridge.

The dust storms, flies and heat were worse than at Orange River. Enteric was rampant, and altogether it was a most pestilential place. Beyond occasionally taking sick convoys down to Orange River there was little to vary the monotony.

Connacher was attached to the Highland Brigade Field Hospital. Lord Roberts arrived on the [blank], and preparations were made for an advance. Unfortunately Methuen's division was left behind, so we missed Paardeberg, but all the wounded and sick were brought in to us, 3 days' journey in ox waggons. We had 800 in one day, and 300 a day or two afterwards. On this occasion I was down at Modder River drift helping to get them across, and Cronjé, his wife, grandson and secretary were brought in and they passed a few yards from where I was at the drift.

The next day the 4000 prisoners were brought in and kept in a strong barbed wire laager, strongly guarded, till they were transferred to Cape Town.

Among the loose material found in Langmore's diary is a handwritten 'Kos lijs' or menu for the Christmas dinner at Modder River drawn up lightheartedly in an attempt at

South African Dutch. It includes 'Braai fleeshe', 'Rooibeet zli', 'Poring (Xmas)' and 'Jellies and Blaauw Maantz'.

In the course of the general British advance during the early months of 1900, Kimberley was relieved on 15 February, as already described by Elizabeth Atkinson. Cronjé fell back from Magersfontein with a laager of no fewer than 400 ox-wagons encumbered by large numbers of women, children and civilian vehicles. Moving more quickly, Lord Roberts caught up with him at Paardeberg on the Modder River, where he defeated the Boer forces on 18 February and surrounded the laager; it was not until 27 February, however, that Cronjé surrendered. This was a heavy blow to the Republican cause, and a great encouragement to the British.

The day after Cronjé's surrender, Ladysmith was relieved, as described here by J.B. Jardine. The references to Intombi and Buller have already been explained in the previous extract from his diary (p. 31 above); Comdt. Genl. P.J. Joubert of Transvaal was Buller's counterpart on the Boer side.

28th February 1900, Wednesday. Great excitement: three squadrons of the Natal Carabineers arrived this evening at 6.15. We have not got any news of what has happened, but I saw any amount of Boers and waggons retiring all day. 119 days have we sat here, and it is hard to believe that it is all over. The Carabineers came in very solemnly, and must have given great joy to the poor people in Intombi, for they must have passed quite close to their camp. I do hope Buller will get at them and they have a difficult line of retreat, as we practically block the direct line. I think the Boers have waited a bit too long, and it is quite on the cards that they lose most of their baggage and guns at any rate. A thunderstorm this after-noon will make the roads deep for their waggons, thank goodness!

Cronjé captured with his force and Joubert driven to retreat are two good days' news for people at home. What a pity we can't go out and hammer them!

After the initial reverses, the notable British successes in February and March 1900 caused almost disproportionate rejoicing not only in South Africa, but also in Great Britain and throughout the British Empire, and much of the general excitement of this time is conveyed by the diary of Maria Bamberger, a young woman living with her parents at 38 Bird Street, Port Elizabeth. The volume contains irregular entries from 1897, dealing mainly with social occasions, holidays, minor illnesses and, in later years, the distant war; the last reads enigmatically, 'R.H.L. left for the front in K.F.S., 24.11.1901'.

A.N. Bamberger, Maria's father, was a civil servant who had served as Resident Magistrate and Civil Commissioner at Bedford and Hanover, but in 1888 became a railway accountant in Port Elizabeth. Among the papers of J.H. Hofmeyr there is a letter from James Sivewright, Commissioner for Crown Lands and Public Works, *dated 23 October 1891 in which he informs Hofmeyr, 'Bamberger's matter is finally settled. He will be restored to the bench at an early date.' This does not, however, appear to have happened, so that at almost sixty years of age he may be deemed not to have been a success.*

The Bambergers' social life in Port Elizabeth appears, understandably, to have been predominantly English, and Mrs Bamberger was possibly English-speaking, but Bamberger came from an Afrikaans family, and this may explain his reaction to his daughter's somewhat effusive display of pro-British feelings. The 'victory at Osfontein' probably refers to the battle of Poplar Grove, on the way to Bloemfontein, the British camp being situated at Osfontein. It was followed by the occupation of Bloemfontein on 13 March.

Thursday, 6th March [1900]. After tea there came a knock at the door. I went to see, soon I opened it. Someone nearly fell in and was standing close to the door apparently drunk. Annie next went, but could not make out who it was. Naturally we becamed alarmed and curious, when all at once the supposed drunkard rushed in after us. It was Willie R. He did not leave after all, is only going on Wednesday (tomorrow). We had some music and spent a pleasant evening.

Wednesday, 7th [March]. Willie left early this morning for Barkly [East]. Went tonight to a 'Soldiers' Comforts' concert in the Market Hall, got news of a British victory at Osfontein, near Bloemfontein. We are all delighted!

14th March 1900. Tonight we were awakened by hearing a gun fire and the hooters, steam whistles, etc., the long looked for news has come at last, Bloemfontein has been taken by our troops (Lord Roberts) without a shot being fired!! It is splendid news indeed!

Mother and I got up, I sat on the balcony till one o'clock, Mother sitting by the open window, listening to the cheering, singing, bells, etc. It was a perfect moonlight night, so calm and bright! Amidst all the noise and distant voices we heard the soft cooing of a turtle dove, which sounded like a message of Peace in the calm of the night.

The MacAndrews got dressed and went down town. We got back to bed feeling very restless and excited!

Thursday, 15th [March] 1900. This has been a day never to be forgotten. After breakfast I went to town with the MacAndrews, came home, had something to eat, went down again 1/2 past 11, came home at one! After dinner I asked my Father if he would '*allow*' me to hang a flag over the balcony, whereupon he stormed at me and threatened to strike me, called me most insulting names, [and] got hold of my poor delicate mother by the arm so severely that it has left quite a bruise. O what a coward and *tyranising* tyrant! *Never*, no *never* will I forget this day! Have felt quite ill since.

Went down in the evening again. Came home feeling very tired and sick at heart.

23. 'General Cronje (x) and his officers marching to British camp as prisoners', one of a number of snap-shots of Boer prisoners taken after Cronjé's surrender at Paardeberg on 27 February 1900, from the album of A.J. Oke. (INIL 2235)

Cruel world, and still more cruel parent!

(. . .)

April 14th, Monday. Went down town this morning. Evening went over to Bidens, found Mr Atmore alone at home with the boys. Lovely night, calm and bright as usual. Feeling very happy tonight.

Wednesday, 16th April 1900. Went with Mr Burness to the theatre tonight – Lilliputians played *The Gondoliers*. It was a bright moonlight night. Enjoyed myself very much indeed as usual.

Thursday, 13th Sep. 1900. Maud Jones, Father and self went to a Grand Masonic Ball in Feather Market. M. and I enjoyed ourselves very much indeed. I danced all evening, came home and went in a carriage.

The long-delayed relief of Mafeking on 17 May was to cause near-hysteria, although this is not covered by Maria Bamberger's diary, where there are only two further entries for 1900. It was followed by the British occupation of Johannesburg on 31 May and Pretoria on 5 July, and later that month by another spectacular British success, when Genl. A.M. Prinsloo of the Bethlehem commando was surrounded in the Brandwater Basin in the eastern Free State, on the border of what was then Basutoland, and obliged to surrender with close on 5000 men. In The Times History of the War *this is called 'one of the greatest military achievements of the war'.*

Prinsloo's surrender is described here in an extract from the diary of Captain R.B. Pott of the West Kent Yeomanry. Like the letters of J.B. Jardine, the diary was typed out and bound after the war, and it is moreover illustrated by almost 300 snapshots taken by Pott himself. Although many of the latter are not very good, the diary and photographs together form a unique record of the eighteen months Pott spent in South Africa, mainly in this part of the Free State during the period of guerrilla warfare.

Sunday, 29th July 1900. A great day. Reveille at 4.45 a.m. Orders to have everything packed by 6 a.m. Stood to until 2 p.m. Heard that the Boers were trying to make terms with Gen. Hunter.

Marched at 2.p.m. about two miles to a fresh camp, heard on the way that the Boers had surrendered, but feared it was only the usual camp rumour. On arriving in camp, however, the following message was signalled through the flags, 'Five thousand Boers surrendered to-day unconditionally at 4 p.m. and are now coming into camp.' This is believed to be the whole force now before us.

The Leinster band went to Head-quarters and played 'Soldiers of the Queen' and the National Anthem, the whole camp joining in. Cheers were long, loud and continuous. It was a great sight.

There are some 20 000 now encamped here (Caledon River valley); the camp extends up the valley and is about four or five miles long.

I personally celebrated the event by drinking eternal confusion to all Boers, in whisky, of which we have but one bottle left. I also laid a brother officer £25 to £5 that we eat our Christmas Dinner in England.[1] The Mess table was chopped up for firewood in the excitement.

Now comes the question what orders will the Imperial Yeomanry get. 'Is it England or the Transvaal?' To-morrow will probably show.

The combined columns of Rundle, Clements and Hunter are here. I was in command of the West Kent Squadron to-day owing to Mills being ill, he having caught a chill on the night of the 25th.

The Basutos lit bonfires all along the border heights to celebrate the Boer surrender.

Monday, 30th July 1900. Another great day. I was detailed to take the Squadron, with the exception of 15 men, to escort Boer prisoners to Fouriesburg. Paraded at 6.45 a.m. and reported myself at Gen. Hunter's camp at 7.30 a.m. Waited about half a mile back for the first batch. The scene was a fine one: on the top of a high flat hill

---

1. Note in the original: 'I did not win this bet.'

24. 'Prinsloo's surrender', Brandwater Basin, 30 July 1900, a snapshot from the album of R.B. Pott. (INIL 9990)

(now called Surrender Hill) was planted the Union Jack. Generals Hunter, Rundle, Clements and Paget beneath it received the Boer prisoners, consisting of the Ficksburg commando and the Ladybrand commando, each 500 strong.

There was some hitch early in the day, a representative coming from the Boer laager to demand terms. General Hunter gave him half an hour to surrender, and trained all the British guns on the Boer laager. This decided the matter, and at 11 o'clock the Ficksburg commando came in. They passed through lines of infantry consisting of Scots Guards, Leinster and West Kent Regiments (whose bands had been playing alternately during the morning), and threw down their arms before passing the Generals. These arms were broken up on an anvil. The Boer officers were allowed to give up their rifles to the Generals.

About 3 p.m. the names of the prisoners, the description of their rifles and the number of their ponies had been taken, and they were ready for the escort. General Rundle came up at that moment, and asking for the officer in command of the escort, informed me that I was to place a man with a loaded rifle on each side of a certain Field Cornet, and if one single prisoner attempted to escape, the Field Cornet was to be shot. He was to be responsible to me on arrival at Fouriesburg for 200 burghers. This the Field Cornet declined, so the whole were detained for the night, guarded by the Leinster Regiment. Each Boer was allowed to retain one pony (his worst), and several Cape carts and ox waggons were allowed to go with them.

Rum was served out to the troops to-night, and festivities, songs etc. were the order of the evening. I had an interesting conversation with a Field Cornet. Many of the men were glad to be prisoners instead of having to fight, and the Field Cornet told me that he could not get more than a quarter of his men to go into the positions allotted to them during the last week, they being tired of fighting.

The feelings of the Boers and their sympathisers in the winter of 1900 may be conveyed by quoting from a letter written by Jacoba Lorentz shortly after the occupation of Pretoria. The writer was a well-educated Dutchwoman who had come to the Transvaal with her family in the 1870s and seems to have identified herself closely with the country and its people. [Translation on pp. 150-151.]

Pretoria, 6 Juni 1900

Lieve Trui, – Eindelijk is de slag gevallen en zijn wij Engelsch. Gisteren kwamen er een 50 000 troepen binnen en namen bezit van de stad. Gelukkig ging alles zeer rustig en ordelijk toe. De soldaten toonden door blik noch gebaar hunne vreugde, en gedroegen zich uiterst bescheiden en voorkomend waar zij in aanraking kwamen met het publiek. Zoo had men het ook verwacht van eene beschaafde natie, doch er hadden zooveel vreeselijke verhalen in de courant gestaan van wangedrag der soldaten, vooral tegenover vrouwen, dat wij met angst hunne komst tegemoetzagen en vele vrouwen zich gewapend hadden om zich bij afwezigheid der mannen te kunnen verdedigen tegenover een opgewonden en woeste bende, zooals de soldaten ons waren afgeschilderd.

Gelukkig is alles in de beste orde geschied. Stil en rustig bezetten zij de straten en defileerden over het Kerkplein. Lord Roberts kwam ook heel onopgemerkt binnen, en geen muziek of voor ons kwetsend vreugdebetoon werd gehoord of gezien, en eerst laat op de dag werd de Engelsche vlag geheeschen op het Goevernementsgebouw. Die is mij een doorn in het oog, meer dan ik zeggen kan. De oorlog is geheel en al onrechtvaardig, en de Engelschen hebben ons eenvoudig het onze ontstolen; men kan geene andere uitlegging geven aan deze annexatie. En als men daarover nadenkt, komt iemands gemoed in opstand over zooveel onrechtvaardigheid. Hoe is het mogelijk, hebben wij in de laatste maanden herhaaldelijk uitgeroepen, dat God aldus het onrecht laat zegevieren. De handeling der Engelschen schreit ten hemel en roep om wraak. (. . .)

It is only fair to add that Jacoba Lorentz goes on in this letter to write with some indig-

25. 'Louis Botha addressing burghers in Church Square, Pretoria, 30th May [1900], announcing British defeat [sic], Johannesburg.' The view is from the balcony of the Grand Hotel across the Square, with the towers of the Palace of Justice visible behind the church. (From, The Earl of Rosslyn: Twice Captured)

nation about the corruption of the Republican Government which was brought to light after the flight of President Kruger and the occupation of the town by the British.

A graphic account of the western campaign which had brought the British forces from the Orange River to Pretoria within six months is to be found in a letter written by Private Percy Cogle of the North Somerset Yeomanry. It is one of four letters to 'Cliff' or 'Clifford' which during the the course of 1900 were successively sent from Las Palmas, Edenburg, Pretoria and Bloemfontein; they are preceded by an undated letter from the 'London Dining Rooms, Upper Borough Walls, Bath' in which he announces his departure for South Africa, with the injunction, 'Mind you write to me out there, you know what letters are out there, a dam site [sic] better than a good feed very often.'

By the time Cogle found himself at Edenburg, Bloemfontein had been occupied, but Roberts had been obliged to remain there for a few weeks in order to allow his troops to recuperate. During this period the southern Free State was subjugated, with some

26. 'British troops entering Pretoria, June 5th, 1900', with the station buildings in the background. (Cape Times Weekly, 11.7.1900)

resistance on the part of the Boers, Edenburg surrendering on 25 March. It was not until the end of April that the march northwards was resumed: in his next letter Cogle would be able to describe the occupation of Pretoria.

Sir William Gatacre, mentioned by Cogle, had been deprived of his command after having proved to be an ineffectual commander in the Stormberg area and the southern Free State,

Edenburg, South Africa, April 16/00

Dear Cliff, – Very pleased to receive your letter before leaving Cape Town. Well now, I'll start from the time of landing at that place.

We stood off the harbour for three days, after which we landed, and from that time we started work in earnest. We were all day and about half the night unloading with three cranes going all the time. The next morning we got the horses off and rode to Maitland Camp, almost five miles from Cape Town, where there were about ten thousand troops, a part of almost every regiment of the British Army, and also a party of all the Colonial troops. After staying there for fifteen days were were ordered to this place, which you will see on the map is about forty miles from Bloemfontein, and after staying here for three days for the horses to rest we shall march straight on. It is about three days' journey for us, because we have to go very careful owing to the rebels about here.

It took us three days and three nights to get here by train from Cape Town, and after passing Naauw Poort we saw all the places the Boers had taken and afterwards [been] driven from. All the way at intervals of about five miles were guards of about thirty men. We passed plenty of Boer prisoners going down to the base, and on Wednesday morning we saw Gen. Gatacre and his servant on their way back. Of course you know he is recalled.

The Canadians have just arrived in this camp after marching about thirty miles to-day, and we have a company of the Grenadiers just by us. This morning the Colonel came to us and told us that he was very sorry we were leaving the other three Companies of the battalion, but he had just received orders that the 48th Company (that is, ours) were chosen by Lord Roberts as his bodyguard of Imperial Yeomanry. He said it was a very great honour indeed, but what the work is I'm sure I do not know any more than the man in the moon. But perhaps you will hear of this in the papers much sooner than you get this.

I say, if this is correct, won't it be a blue ribbon day for the North Somerset Yeomanry? I can tell you the Devons, Dorsets, West Somersets (the other three Companies of our Battalion) are jolly savage about it, and so is the rest of the Imperial troops. I think Major Sherston, our Major, arranged it for us, because he was in communication with Roberts ever since we landed, and he is a nephew of his.

I gave my cord vest to Willie before leaving or you should have had it. Vowles, Marshall and Blackmore wish to be remembered to you (all well). I say, Charlie or George Payne do not know I'm out here, at least not from me, and I hope they have not told them from home, just Janey calling on them all on the hop. (What, off she bumps.)

Ever since leaving Maitland Camp we have had only biscuits and bully beef. The biscuits are square and about the size of a dog biscuit and for all the world like them, as hard as a board. I should like to have just one good meal (for fun, you know). Good Friday we spent in the train, and today (Monday) we are working jolly hard. We were saying we bet you were in our place this morning talking about us (not far wrong, eh?). I can tell you we thought about you dinnertime on Sunday. Should have liked to have changed places for about one hour. We were putting up tents and cleaning kit all day, and did not get anything to eat or drink from seven in the morning until five in the evening, but what odds, it all comes in the day's work, and we do not care as long as we get it some time or the other.

You must excuse this sheet of note paper, it's getting scarce and we have no kit bags, having all been left at the base. We do not get any news here, and you get it a jolly good time quicker and more correct than they get it out here at all. They think more of London news at the Cape than if it came down country.

I've met several people from Weston here, Sam Stradling the coal merchant's son and young Norman the grocer's son (Regent Street). Things are very expensive out here. Cheese 1/9 per lb. that I would not eat if I were home, (beastly) butter 2s., and a tin of condensed milk 1/6, bread you have a hard job to get at all. I will try and get you some Kruger money if I can. We have not seen very much as yet, everyone seems to be after it, you have to give 2s. for a sixpence and 30s. for a sovereign, but I expect we shall be able to get plenty up country.

Now you must write another jolly good long letter next time, as I would just as soon have one from you (as a good dinner). We shall have been under fire, I expect, by the time it arrives. You must excuse this scribble, as I am writing this on my knee with a candle stuck on a tin in the tent, which is writing under difficulties, I think, and not having any more news to tell you, [*some words illegible*] to a close, hoping that this will find you in the best of health and spirits, and believe me, your ever affectionate pal, Percy Cogle.

P.S. Please remember me kindly to all your people.

The account of the British advance is continued by Ford S. Barclay, an officer in Kitchener's Horse (3rd South African Light Horse), an irregular corps raised in the Cape Colony. The world he came from, the military circles in which he moved and the vocabulary he employed differ very obviously from those of Percy Cogle, and the envelope accompanying his letter is addressed to Sir Reginald Beauchamp, Bart., Langley Park, Beccles, Suffolk. Both letter and envelope are badly stained and apparently also scorched, making parts of the text difficult to read, and the envelope has been stamped 'Recovered from mails looted by the enemy'. In June 1900, C.R. de Wet, who had newly come to prominence as a military leader, was harassing the British forces in the northern Free State in the vicinity of the railway line between Johannesburg and Kroonstad.

During the early months of the war, Barclay had served under Col. H.H. Settle, who was engaged in subduing the rebellious districts of the northern Cape. 'Sana's Post' and 'Cronstadt' are Sannapos (to the east of Bloemfontein) and Kroonstad respectively. Welkom Drift on the Vet River was secured by the British on 4 May, Roberts forced a passage through the Sand River on 10 May, and Kroonstad was occupied two days later. By 'Heilbron Junction' Barclay probably meant Vredefort Road (modern Koppies); Elandsfontein is the modern Germiston, and 'Vereenigan' is Vereeniging.

With all Barclay's enthusiasm about 'a pretty little piece of shooting' and the wounded portion of the 'bag' being laid out 'in the most approved style', it is hard to keep in mind that it is the killing of men he is describing. Even the reference to ground 'literally covered with blood' might as well refer to a successful day's hunting.

In hospital, Johannesburg
8th June 1900

My dear Beauchamp, – I have been meaning to write to you for some time, but since leaving Bloemfontein on the 26th April we have been kept so constantly busy I could find no time for it. All the mounted infantry have been kept pretty well on the run, and Kitchener's Horse, especially my squadron, have had rather more than our fair share.

27. 'On the move', from the Pott Album. (INIL 9881)

Our first bit of soldiering was to march to Prieska under Kitchener, and later on to Uppington under an old dotard named Settle. From there fortunately we were ordered to join the Regiment at Bloemfontein and marched in there about April 20th. Up to here we had seen no real fighting, though a few sniping shots had been loosed at us near Uppington.

On the 26th we got orders to march in 1 1/2 hours to Sana's Post on a two days' reconnaissance. We were to leave all Transport behind and take nothing but what we could carry on our horses. Of course we had our suspicion about the two days, and sure enough we never saw our Transport again till we had taken Cronstadt on the 10th!

Our first objective point was Thabanchu, in going away from which on the 29th I had my first baptism of fire. We caught it pretty hot, and of the two squadrons engaged lost three officers killed and two wounded, but the men did splendidly and, though ontnumbered about 8-1, the beggars couldn't oust us and we held the position till relieved by the Gordons at 2 o'clock the next morning.

Most of the fighting here, as well as at the two subsequent fights at Hout Nek and Welkom's Drift, was done at close range, as close at times indeed that we were hurling anathemas at one another's heads between the shots! At Hout Nek my squadron was only under rifle fire for a few minutes, but it was pretty hot while it lasted, one of my troop actually shooting a chap from the hip, as he hadn't got time to raise his rifle to the shoulder.

Welkom's Drift was really our show fight! The Regiment was only about 120 strong that morning, but we were sent forward to take a ridge held by 150 Boers in order to get the Household Cavalry out of a mess (poor young Rose of the Blues was killed in it). We had to advance over 300 yards of bare plain, a pom-pom giving us hell on our right front, a 'Long Tom' on our flank, and on our left front, beyond the Household Cavalry but sheltered from their fire, a Maxim and about 50 of the enemy's sharp shooters! It looked a pretty formidable task, and what made it worse was that before we started we had had ample time to take in all the worst points about it with our glasses!

We advanced in columns of troops at the trot, ten paces' interval between each man, and though the old hands said it was the hottest fire they had ever been under, especially as we neared the ridge, we had only one man hit. It turned out afterwards that fourteen horses were wounded, but as only two fell, we knew nothing of it until we came back to them again after taking the position.

Legge, our Colonel, luckily spotted a sort of bay in the range of hills where we could dismount almost entirely under cover, so we were able to form up for the final act without any bothering bullets flying about. Then, each troop leader giving the word, we started up the ridge. About 50 of the beggars had the cheek to stand their ground, and when we got to the top we had about five minutes plugging at one another at under 50 yards' sweep. We had [word illegible], so couldn't charge properly, and we had all our work cut out to keep our men down under cover, they would keep standing up to get a better view!   Two or three of the enemy, Germans as they eventually turned out to be, tried the same game on, but always went down almost as soon as they showed themselves – I know I got in some pretty useful work with my carbine!!

At last they bolted, and we had as pretty a little piece of shooting as they ran down to their horses as I ever hope to see! Our squadron as their share of the bag, the wounded portion of which was all laid out in a row in the most approved style, claimed eleven, besides three killed and four prisoners, including a Field Cornet! Our own losses in the actual charge were one officer and three men killed and three wounded, so we got off fairly cheap. We afterwards heard that not more than half a dozen of the enemy who actually stayed to the end actually escaped without a wound, and I think it very probable as, as long as we could see them galloping off over the veldt, men kept falling from their horses and had to be helped on again by their friends.

Sand River, our next show, proved one of the most decisive of the war. Our losses were very small, I heard under fifty, but from all *their* accounts heard from the prisoners they must have lost terribly; at any rate they haven't made a real stand since. The Artillery fire was wonderful, and from what men who were at both fights say, much more effective than at Paardeburg. Our men discovered where the horses belonging to some of the enemies'[?] guns were and turned six batteries on to them. There happened to be, as we could see from our position, about 1000 Boers just dismounted, probably going into the firing line as reinforcement to the escort of their guns, so you can imagine the effect of the first 20 or 30 shells bursting within 5 seconds of one another and all splendidly placed! I rode to the place next morning and the ground was literally covered with blood, though the infantry who were first up after the shelling told me told me they only found three bodies lying there. It certainly is a mystery how they get their dead and wounded away!

After Kroonstadt we expected a bit of a rest, but were ordered away again with Hamilton's Division to visit Lindley and Heilbron, where we heard a lot of the enemy were concentrating. We were twelve days on the job and every day had more or less skirmishing, but for some reason the General wouldn't stop to give them the smashing they wanted. The report was that he was leaving them for Rundle, but as he was at least a week behind us, goodness only knows how their forces may have grown when he comes up.

My squadron was left behind on the railway at Heilbron Junction to escort a convoy of 54 waggons to Elandsfontein. We were dreadfully sick about it at the time, as some heavy fighting was expected at all the drifts over the Vaal; however, as it turned out, we had a much more exciting time, as about 200 Boers were hovering about on our right flank and kept us very much on the qui vive until we reached Vereenigan. Some niggers told us there were over a thousand within 8 miles of the road, and if it's true it speaks volumes for the effect of the last three weeks' fighting that they should have funked attacking a small force of at the outside 75 men. It's true the road was all along open country and they had no [*word illegible*], still I think that the Dopper Boer would have attacked a month ago if the disparity in numbers had been so great. Twenty-three of them actually withdrew before our outside flankers consisting of only four men!

I suppose things will get through all right with the usual luck of the British Army, but they are employing a lot of raw Yeomanry as escort to a good many convoys, and goodness only knows what would happen if they allowed themselves to be surprised!

The last few days before arriving here were perfect hell for me, as I had been suffering for three weeks with dysentery and I kept falling off my horse from sheer weakness. We had no ambulance, so I simply had to keep on, and I finally marched in with Roberts' force more dead than alive. Fortunately they do you very well here, and I am now able to sit up in bed, so hope to be with the Regiment in a fortnight or so.

There are all sorts of rumours flying about, chiefly pointing to the early finish of the war. I'm afraid though it will be at least another four months before any of us will be able to start home. And I shouldn't be much surprised if we didn't get the job over by Xmas. Yrs very truly, Ford S. Barclay.

28. 'Gen. Pole-Carew commanding 11th Division, watching troops and transports crossing the Vet River, S.A.', one of a number of stereograph views of the British advance from Bloemfontein to Pretoria in the winter of 1900. (Underwood & Underwood)

That the war had been concluded with the occupation of the Boer Republics, and that operations only needed to be rounded off by disposing of the odd commandoes still in the field, was a general perception among the British. By the winter of 1900 conditions had been stabilised to such an extent that Theo Schreiner was able to undertake a tour of the Orange River battlefields, scenes of such violent fighting only six months before.

Schreiner, who was the brother of the former Prime Minister, W.P. Schreiner, and of Mrs Stakesby Lewis, both of whom have already been quoted, was fervently pro-British and a personal friend of Cecil Rhodes. At this time he enjoyed considerable standing in South Africa as a temperance preacher and leader of the Good Templar organisation, in which he enjoyed the close co-operation of his widowed niece, Mrs Katie Stuart, a remarkably gifted woman in her own right. The following is taken from a long account by Mrs Stuart of Schreiner's visit to the battlefields, on which she accompanied him with her young son Donald. It was composed by her at Modder River, Belmont and Grahamstown towards the end of June 1900, and subsequently typed out, presumably for circulation in the extensive Schreiner family circle. The South African Library holds both an incomplete carbon copy, and a complete manuscript transcription of the original, seemingly made by a child.

The extract below describes an expedition undertaken from Belmont on 28 June to the site of the battle in which the Boers had been driven back on 28 November 1899, early in the British advance towards Kimberley. The 'Nannie' to whom reference is made was

29. 'Lord Roberts (3d to left) and escort of Imperial Yeomanry, entering Kroonstadt, Boer War, S.A.', another in the extensive series of stereograph views of the war issued by the publishing firm Underwood & Underwood of London and the United States. (Underwood & Underwood)

Ettie Stakesby Lewis's maid and companion, Anna Tempo, later to become well known as a social worker in her own right under the name 'Sister Nannie'. 'Aunt Olive' was, of course, Olive Schreiner, but it is not clear to which of her pronouncements on the war the woman with the 'cold, steely eyes' was referring.

(. . .) Theo had set his heart on our exploring all the important kopjes, and also of visiting the Boer laager behind the kopjes which the British burnt that glorious day when they chased the Boers from kopje to kopje with ringing cheers and demonstrated for ever that the Boer safely entrenched behind boulders or on top of a kopje cannot withstand the dash of British valour.

There was a larger laager further on, towards Graspan, which the British also captured and destroyed, but we had no time to visit it. Only a few weeks ago soldiers going to the laager had been sniped at, and there was just enough spice of risk attached to our going to make it delightful.

We got a pass from the British officer in command, though it was not at all necessary, and after getting it we felt that it was the most dangerous thing we could have about us should we fall into rebel hands, so I hid it carefully in the lining of my bodice.

Finding that Mr De Kock was willing to hire us his cart and horses for 10s., we

30. 'Difficulties of transport', a snapshot from the Pott Album. (INIL 9975)

engaged it. I confess I felt a bit nervous at first and thought of Nannie's dread lest the Boers should shoot Theo; but we found nothing to alarm us anywhere. We drove to the south or right of the kopjes held by the Boers and which our soldiers so bravely charged and took, and truly one marvelled at their bravery and courage as one gazed at the steep sides and later on scrambled with difficulty up them, over huge black boulders.

The Boers had been entrenched in the whole block, a triangle of kopjes about 5 by 4 by 3 miles. We drove around the 5 miles' side where the British attacked to the laager around the other side near a large homestead. Leaving the cart, a short walk brought us to the laager where 24 wagons [were] drawn up in a very small valley in three rows of seven each and three evidently commandants' wagons, thus: [*small diagram*]. Every bit of woodwork and canvas was burnt, only the iron skeletons remain. We gathered some exploded cartridges and quaint lumps of melted glass, evidently castor oil and other bottles, and a padlock off a forekist.

Returning to the cart we then, after consultation, decided to drive up to the homestead and visit the farmers there. The feelings aroused in one's heart by the Boers' treachery in having thus invaded the Colony and being encouraged thereto by the rebels made us shrink from going; but only that morning God's spirit had made us feel how incumbent it was upon us as representatives of the conquering race never to omit

31. 'A midday halt', from the Pott Album. (INIL 10102)

a single instance of shaking hands with a Boer or of speaking a kindly word, that the breach might be healed up, so we went and we were so glad afterwards.

The old man called Van Eijck was at the kraals with three other younger men, as as we drove up to the house he todd[l]ed up to see us. A bevy of roaring and formidable dogs greeted us, and then a bevy of young girls, all about 14 to 16 years of age. I asked in Dutch whether the dogs would bite, and the mere sound of Dutch brought a welcome on their faces, and we were kindly invited in and presented with a delicious cup of tea each. They called the girls *vluchtelings* who had gathered there because of the war from neighbouring farms. They said that four households were on the farm.

The old man told us how on the day of the battle he took refuge with 23 women and children in the kraals, where stray bullets now and then came, for fear of a shell bringing the house down upon them, but that his poor wife, a bedridden sufferer from cancer, was left in her bed. The house was unscathed. The old man by his telling of his being in charge of 23 women and children let the cat out of the bag as to where the able-bodied men all were.

They were all eager for peace save one woman, his daughter, of about 30 years of age, whose cold, steely eyes and whole demeanour bespoke revenge and brought Aunt Olive's words to mind. She asked me to see her mother and say a word of comfort, as the poor old soul was in great spiritual darkness and conflict. I was helped, and so was Theo, to deal with the case, and we offered up earnest prayers for them all. After we left, however, I felt as if I had perhaps missed the point where the poor old woman had to be helped, i.e. her sin as a quiet, peaceful subject of the Queen's to have helped and sympathized with rebellion. It was nice to find that the unique power of getting on with and influencing the Boers which God has granted us in the past is ours yet.

The woman with the cold, steely eyes wanted to know if Aunt Olive was Theo's sister.

In October of that year Theo Schreiner was to be one of the delegates sent to Britain by the South African Vigilance Committee 'for the purpose of enlightening the British public as to the state of affairs in South Africa, and strengthening the hands of the Home Government in its South African policy'; Mrs Stuart accompanied him as representative of the Loyal Women's Guild. They were to spend almost a year in Britain, campaigning vigorously for the pro-war party in the face of mounting criticism of the war.

32. (opposite). 'Brabant's Horse crossing the bridge at Aliwal North on the journey to the relief of Wepener'; a photograph by A. Dugmore (detail). The Free State town of Wepener, which was besieged by the Boers, was relieved on 8 October 1900. (Cape Times Weekly, 10.10.1900)

SETTLING IN
(LATE 1900)

I '*shouldn't be much surprised if we didn't get the job over by Xmas,*' *F. S. Barclay remarked in his letter written from Johannesburg in the winter of 1900 (p. 59 above), and the sentiment seemed reasonable enough. The Boer capitals had been occupied and the Orange Free State was formally annexed on 24 May, while the annexation of Transvaal was to follow on 1 September. September likewise saw the retreat of President Kruger over the border to Lourenço Marques (Maputo), Carolina, Barberton and Lydenburg were occupied by the British and Schweizer-Reneke and Ladybrand relieved, and Lord Roberts issued a proclamation calling on the Boers to surrender.*

The following documents reflect the situation during the second half of 1900, in what seemed to the British merely a time for consolidating their victory.

By the late winter of 1900, the civil surgeon H.R. Langmore, who had been at Modder River in December (see pp. 44-46 above), found himself stationed on a farm near Olifantsnek in the Magaliesberg, with a great deal of sporadic fighting under Methuen and Baden-Powell going on around him. 'The country here is very pretty and fertile', he noted in his diary. 'We are driving the Boers in front of us, and heavy fire from our field pieces and pom-poms is proceeding, also rapid rifle fire. Got some tea and rusks at a Boer farm, also a lot of violets.' He often went bathing in the nearby river.

The following is an arbitrary extract from Langmore's diary for this period. In the previous month already Methuen had been ordered by Roberts to denude the Western Transvaal of horses, cattle and supplies in an attempt to break the lingering Boer resistance, which explains the nature of the expedition he accompanied. The B.S.A. were the British South African Police, and 'R.N.L.' according to Dr Arthur Davey is a faulty abbreviation for the Loyal North Lancashires ('Royal' instead of 'Loyal'). By 'pumelloes' he presumably meant 'pompelmoes' or shaddocks, a kind of citrus fruit.

6 [August 1900]. At 8.30 a.m. rode out with Wood and O'Gorman and 25 B.S.A. Police, also a half company of R.N.L. under Major Churchward, to visit some farms. The first (Rickard's) had been looted by the Boers, so we went on and came across a trooper who had lost his way – he had seen earlier in the morning 60 Boers riding up the kloof from a farmhouse further on.

Went on to a second farm which belonged to an old Boer woman who said she was a widow, so this we left alone. The third belonged to a notorious rascal (Conradie). This was searched notwithstanding an indignant and blasphemous female.

33. 'Unveiling C.M.R. memorial, S.A. War, 1899-1902, at East London by Sir Walter Hely-Hutchinson', *an undated photograph probably taken in the immediate aftermath of the war. Hely-Hutchinson was at the time Governor of the Cape Colony, and the memorial commemorated the Cape Mounted Riflemen, a Colonial force.* (PHA)

The furniture was good and the rooms clean, a great contrast to most of the farms we've visited. We removed the livestock and foodstuffs. A Kruger penny and box of matches were my share of the loot. The owners were informed that unless the cattle was driven in by noon tomorrow the house would be burnt.

Only one shot fired at us. We brought back much forage and poultry, etc. The latter were mostly knocked over with oranges and lemons, the pigs were bayonetted.

Got orders at 10 p.m. to move off at once. Put patients into the ambulance waggon, inspanned and moved off in 30 minutes. No lights, no smoking, as the Boers all around. About 5 miles off reached a very bad drift where the waggons stuck. Two only besides mine got across, so bivouacked here for the night. Next morning got a lot of pumelloes from a farm near by.

The situation in which Private James Bell of the Cape Town Highlander Volunteer Regiment found himself at the same time was considerably less pleasant. He was part of the force left behind at Modder River to guard the vitally important railway line to the north, and he must have been there at the time Theo Schreiner and Katie Stuart

67

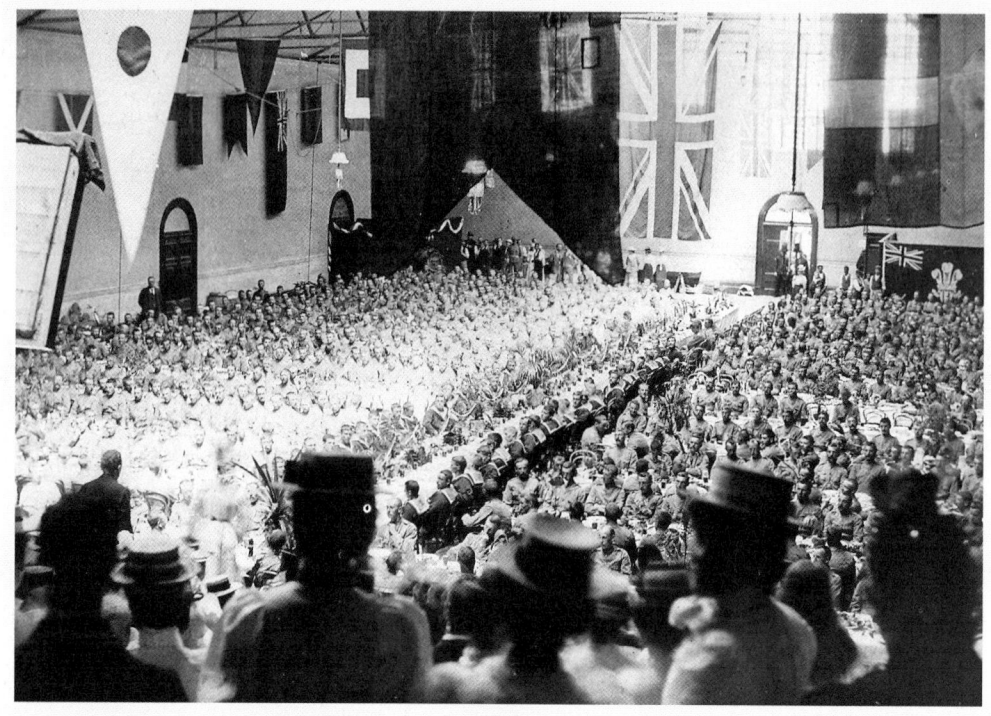

34. Luncheon for the 1st Welsh Regiment, Port Elizabeth: visually one of the most striking Boer War photographs in the collections of the South African Library. (PHA)

were staying at the Crown and Royal Hotel during their visit to the battlefields (see pp. 61-64 above). In her account Mrs Stuart mentioned 'the military small camp' at Modder River, 'just to the right before you reach the bridge. We saw many of them gathered for drill, and when Theo got to Major Lawrie he found him preparing to conduct a short service in the open air for the men, and to our joy Theo was allowed to address them and I closed with prayer. It was a very sweet and unexpected surprise, and God gave us messages of real encouragement to them as Christian warriors and British soldiers.'

James Bell was a Scot, and a number of letters written to members of his family at home have survived; the single envelope which has been preserved is addressed to Mrs Wm Bell, 167 Hospital Street, Glasgow. He led a chequered life, and his letters, covering the period 1900 to 1904 but mainly dealing with the war, were written from various places in South Africa. He was realistic enough in his opinion of the progress of the war, and it is interesting to see his reference to Louis Botha and C.R. de Wet, who were at the time beginning to develop the technique of guerrilla warfare.

Dear Father and Mother, – I have just received your welcome letters, but Sister's has not yet come to hand. I am glad to hear that you are all keeping well and hope that you may continue so. As for myself, I am getting along as well as may be expected, but that it not saying much, a Tommy's life is not all beer and skittles, out here at any rate, however, I'm here and there's no use of growling.

This affair does not seem to be progressing at all, we appear to be as far away from a settlement as ever, this De Wet is giving us a lot of trouble, and until he and Botha are got, there is not much chance of a speedy settlement. We are guarding the lines of communication just now, but are expecting to be sent to Mafeking district shortly.

I am very sorry to hear that you are again at variance with Mr Brown. It does seem a bit tall, his bill in connection with paying the succession duty, but there is probably a reason for it. With regard to the £21[?] surplus, you can send it to me to the following address: James Bell, Poste Restante, Capetown. If the regiment is disbanded (which is very probable) I'll be able to get it there, or if we are not disbanded I can get it forwarded. If sent by either you or Mr Brown, have it registered.

How is Mary and her husband getting along, also Lily and Alexandra? In all the letters I have received there is not much news of them.

I have no fixed idea of what I will do after it is all over, I may come home for a visit or I might go up country again. Each Colonial regiment are sending home a squad of men for parade purposes before the Queen after the thing is all over, and I may stand a chance of getting home and out again, however, I have been recommended by the Captain for the new Transvaal Mounted Police. The pay is 10s. per day and rations, and it will last for six months or so.

I will, however, write you later on every [*word omitted?*] and let you know what I intend doing.

Trusting this will find you all in good health and prosperity. Your affectionate son, James.

By November 1900, Bell was in hospital in Kimberley after 'a bit of a catastrophe': 'I got a Mauser bullet through the upper part of the right arm and another through the muscles of the hip.' He survived the war, however, as will be seen in due course.

Yet another aspect of the war is illustrated vividly in the letters of Lieut. J.H. Kuhlmann of Roberts' Horse, who was also happily making plans for the end of the war and, like Bell, considering a career in the new Transvaal Police. Kuhlmann was a South African by birth, 21 years of age, and before the war had been a leading member of the Gardens Rugby Football team in Cape Town. The letter quoted here was written to his brother: among other things it is revealing in its demonstration of contemporary English slang and clichés and its imitation of upper-class English jargon. This is the way many English-speaking

South Africans wrote, spoke and – as likely as not – thought.

'Heatherley' was in fact Hatherley, Sammy Marks's distillery at Eerste Fabrieken near Pretoria; 'old Berry' has not been traced among the members of the Johannesburg Reform Committee of 1895. Dotty and Toolie were Kuhlmann's sister-in-law and young nephew. 'All Sir Garnet' was a slang expression meaning 'all right': it referred to the British military commander and administrator Sir Garnet Wolseley, who had seen service in many places, including South Africa during the 1870s.

Pretoria, 12/9/00

Dear Jack, – Just a few lines, old boy, to let you know that I'm still kicking, and very strongly too, and only wish that you were feeling as well as I am. There is no doubt about it, this open air life is the very thing to set a fellow up in health, but of course one must be sufficiently strong to be able to stand the hard work and bucketing about one gets while campaigning, especially on this one where we have covered such a tremendous lot of ground. I'm as fit as a fiddler [*sic*] and piling on flesh daily.

I've just come back from Standerton where I went to buy stores, and among other things got 6 c[ase]s Usher's whiskey at 30s. [per] c/s, which is a great advantage on the price we pay here, 15s. per bottle, and then it is only that Heatherley Brewery muck. I met old Berry, the Reform Committee man, and thought him a very decent sort.

Old bean, I've been riding round about the country here, and have come to the conclusion that it will be useless to start farming for some time, as the country is very unsettled and it will require too much capital to start, and then again one can always be on the look out for anything good in that line if you are on the spot. Now there are some awfully good billets going, for instance a Commissioner of Police draws £1000 a year, quarters, rations and horse feed, and if I can tumble into anything like that I shall be perfectly satisfied. I saw Gen. Broadwood and Coln [*sic*] Sinclair, and they are trying to get me fixed up, but I would be awfully glad if you could also manage to do something for me. Do you know anybody in the army up here who would have any influence? If so, please send me a letter of introduction. Or if you know anybody down in Cape Town who has any say, try and get them to write to some influential person here in the form of an introduction. There is no time to be lost over this matter as billets are being filled daily and all by bringing influence to bear; so if you are well enough I would be awfully pleased if you could make a move in the matter as soon as possible.

What do you think of Ruby's intended? Personally I think he is an awfully good little chap and likely to make Ruby a good hubby. I do not know what his prospects are, but from what I have seen I should say he had a very good billet. However, I suppose you will see him about that.

I had a letter from the Mater this morning, and she says George has been bad in hospital, he is not the same man I used to think such a lot of when he was in good

35. 'General Baden Powell and General Brabant in decorated electric car', a photograph taken during the former's official visit to Port Elizabeth in December 1900. (Cape Times Weekly, 23.1.1901)

condition and not soaked thro' and thro' with whiskey.

Give my love to Dottie, also the little 'uns, man, I'm quite anxious to see the little fellows again. I hope they are going strong and Toolie is all Sir Garnet again.

I had quite a long letter from old Joe King. Poor devil, he seems awfully lonely up there, but will soon get used to it I expect. Your affectionate brother, Barge.

Meanwhile Maria Bamberger, still making the best of whatever excitement Port Elizabeth had to offer in wartime, described in her diary how Baden-Powell, the hero of the Siege of Mafeking, was fêted there at the end of 1900. By that time the war was seen to be over: on 11 December, Roberts had departed for England, leaving Kitchener to deal with the last Boer stragglers, and in the House of Commons the Foreign Secretary, Joseph Chamberlain, set out the policy of the British Government with regard to the new South African colonies. On 21 December the Burgher Peace Committee, consisting of men who had laid down their arms and taken the oath of allegiance, met at Pretoria and elected delegates who were to persuade the Boers remaining in the field to surrender.

More significant, however, were the 'terrible war rumours' noted casually by Maria

36. *'The departure of General Buller: General Buller in the act of stepping on the gangway of the Castle liner Dunvegan Castle on his return to England, October 24th, 1900.' Buller had been in command of the Natal Field Force, and his departure signalled the end of the first phase of the war.* (Cape Times Weekly, 31.10.1900)

Bamberger as spoiling her enjoyment of Christmas. Though she obviously did not yet realise it, they meant that the war had by no means ended.

Monday night, 1.20, 12th Nov. 1900. Found a Tommie asleep on one bench on stoep. Father brought him into diningroom, gave him coffee. We were up till three that morning. His name is Leslie, belonged to Thorneycroft's V[olunteer] Corps. Came down on a month's leave. Was staying at the Caledonian Hotel, Main Street. Poor fellow, he was much ashamed of himself.

   24th Dec. 1900. Baden-Powell arrived today, there was great excitement in town. After seeing him on the jetty I came home and got Mother to go and see him in the Park. While there she fainted. I was terribly alarmed, but she got better, and as he went out he pushed through the crowd and shook hands with her! Very kind indeed of him!!

   Mother managed to walk home and laid down on sofa in dining-room. In the evening she was much better, and able to go to the corner of 'Craexus'[?] to see her hero once more in the illuminated tram car. He stood in front on the car, and as he passed her Mother handed him a piece of mistle-toe. He laughed quite loud!! [I] then saw Mother home and went down town with Miss Wheatland and Ethel W.

B.P. is supposed to leave tonight from Graham's Town! Hurrah for the hero and defender of Mafeking!!

25th (Xmas Day) December, 1900. Spent a very quiet but happy day in spite of all the terrible war rumours. Did not go to church. Evening Father and I went for a walk round the Park.

After tea while we were sitting on the stoep we suddenly heard firing and naturally were much alarmed. It was only a gun boat in the bay putting off rockets.

There are all kinds of rumours about, the Boers are in the Colony once more and are threatening several places, horrible devils! No peace while they live.

Sunday morning, 30th Dec. 1900. Jack came back today! Lieut. Coldrey is with him, they look very well. Saw them this afternoon.

Went to church with Father this evening. After church Willie Rousseau came over. Revd. Carey preached tonight.

The MacRoberts are staying at Uitenhage. Not going to Nora's wedding. She will be married in the 3rd Jan. I am awfully disappointed, but it is quite the usual thing for *me*. Nothing but *dull*, dull, monotonous days and a lonely life!

A more cynical view of life away from the front – in this case well away from the front – is to be found in the diary-letters of Captain B.J. Jones of the 1st Leinster Regiment, who only arrived in South Africa in May 1900 and was still in Cape Town at the time he made the following entry. Like the letters of J.B. Jardine and the diary of R.B. Pott, his Boer War letters were subsequently typed out and bound.

The Mount Nelson Hotel in Cape Town had been completed in 1899, just in time for the war, and was very popular with aristocratic or socially ambitious onlookers who had been attracted to South Africa by the excitement.

16th July 1900. Some of the local papers have been rather amusing lately at the expense of the 'Mount Nelson garrison' as they call the fashionable people who inhabit the Mount Nelson Hotel here. Rightly or wrongly the male part of the 'garrison' are not supposed to be very eager for a life of outpost duty and quarter rations up country. The last time Kitchener was down here he visited all the hotels and sent everyone who was not doing duty here back to the front. Nowadays, however, there are comparatively few people at the Mount Nelson, most of the fashionables have gone home, but by all accounts it was a lively place some months ago. One of the few remaining members of the *'haute noblesse'* tried to go up to Pretoria the other day, but was stopped 'by order' in the station. She clamoured, and eventually the authorities agreed to let her go, but not her maid. The offer was of course refused, and the railway staff officer had a very bad quarter of an hour.

Sir Ralph Williams, newly appointed Resident Commissioner to what was then still Bechuanaland Protectorate (Botswana), who arrived in Cape Town a few weeks later, gives much the same impression: 'Of all wonderful sights,' he wrote later in his memoirs, 'the famous Mount Nelson Hotel was one of the most strange, packed as it was with officers from the front and their wives and friends, a medley of people, distinguished and undistinguished, all interested in one subject only, the war.'

Captain Jones left Cape Town for the front before the end of July, and spent the remainder of the war in the north-eastern Free State, in much the same area as that covered by Pott's diary (see further pp. 104-106 below).

37. (opposite). 'School – W.H.F.A. & Sister Champley'; a snapshot by the Quaker Lawrence Richardson showing his companion W.H.F. Alexander during a visit to the Winburg concentration camp on 14 October 1902 (detail). The war had ended some months before, but all the civilians removed from the farms had not yet returned home. (INIL 10416)

THE VANQUISHED
(1902)

*T*he war was to continue for two years after the occupation of the Boer Republics, and henceforth it would involve not only the burghers on commando, but the entire civilian population as well, both white and black. It was the burghers who were captured in battle or surrendered who first experienced the implications of defeat. By December 1900 Boer prisoners of war numbered some 15 000, and there were 37 000 at the end of the war. Commonly these prisoners were transported to Cape Town or Durban by train, pending transmission to a prisoner-of-war camp abroad.

In the Cape, some prisoners were held at Simon's Town, but a large camp arose on what was then still the open ground of Green Point Common. Life here is described in a letter from P.A. Geldenhuis, who would appear to have been from the Heilbron district of the Free State and to have been captured during the early stages of guerrilla warfare. No more is known of him, however: his letter, written to his wife, is one of a small set of Boer War letters found among the papers of Dominee H.C. Hopkins, an indefatigable collector of historical ephemera. It is largely self-explanatory, but the reference to rumours of 'various families having been sent away' should be noted. [Translation on pp. 151-152.]

Groenepunt, 8/1/1901

Waarde en lieve frouw, – Door Gods goedheid zyn wy nog allen redelyk wel in wens u allen het zelfde. Lieve vrouw, het is nu al een geruime tyd dat ik laats van u iets gehoort heef, ik hoor van verscheie famieljes wat weg gestuur is, zoo dat ik zeer nuews schierig is wat van u geworde is.

Zwager Magiel en Frederik en Corneles Taljaart is nog by my, ook Stoffel Nagel, de ander bekende is meeste alger weg gestuur. Papa en Mathys Taljaard is in Zalon aan gekomen. Ik heef van broeder Mathys een brief uit St Helena ont vang gedateerd 13 Dec., toen heef het hem nog goed gegaan.

Ik gevoel my nu zoo gezont als toen ik zo pas getroud was, ik het nu alle morgens een koude bad in het doet my zeer goed. Het is jammer dat ik de zeewater aldag moet zien in niet in de zelfe kan baai. Ons ete in drinke kan ik niet over klagen.

Wat het geestelyk leven betref, het gaan naar de omstandig heid zeer goed, wy het hier al dag Kerk, eers geleid door ds. du Toit in door ds. Aleit, hy heef een maal op Heilbron voor ons gepreek. Ook Mr Spreth preek voor ons, in hy doet het zeer goed. Hier is voor een week gel[e]den over de 400 kinders lidmaat geworden, waar

76

38. 'Prisoners of Cronjé's commando going aboard the transport': Boer prisoners of war taken after the surrender of General Cronjé at Paardeberg on 27 February 1900, being transferred from the camp at Green Point to that at Simon's Town on the transport City of Cambridge. *Most of them were ultimately sent to St Helena.* (Cape Argus Weekly, 30.5.1900)

onder ook P.A. Badenhors is. Cornelis Taljaard was toen ziek, een zweer in zyn oor, anders was [hy] ook klaar. Hy leer nu weer vluks.

Jan Scheepers van oom Lukas is ook hier, als u kan dan moet [u] vir zyn vrouw laat weet het gaan hun nog goed.

Zoo blyk ik na minzaam groete u heilwenschend ech[t]genoot, P. A. Geldenhuis.

U moet myn naam vol uit schryf op myn adres. Als u schryf dan moet [het?] wees: Krygsgevangene te Groenepunt, Kamp no.1, C.C.

The South African Library holds an interesting little set of manuscripts known as the 'Prisoner of War Petitions Collection' which was bought from Sotheby's in 1981. It con-sists mainly of letters written in the camp at Green Point and on board the Bavarian *to Colonels West and Money, the Camp Commandants, as well as two Christmas cards, a water-colour drawing of a prisoner's tent and a potato-cut plan of the camp. Many of these letters request favours, but the writers' motives were very mixed indeed, as may*

39. *A striking but slightly damaged photograph of unidentified Boer prisoners of war on board ship; it was taken by Alf Hosking of Cape Town.* (PHA)

be seen from the following three examples. All three were written in English, and their spelling has been left unchanged.

P. J. de Beer appears to have been a Free State burgher, although his part in the early stages of the war was somewhat less than heroic; he refers to the Free State by its newly acquired name of Orange River Colony. Jagersfontein Road was the modern Trompsburg in the southern Free State.

Green Point, Camp 2, 21st May 1901

Colonel Money, Green Point
Camp 1, Cape Town

Sir, – I'm now P.O.W. for nearly 14 months and wish with your permission to express my opinion.

I'll admit that I deserve my punishment and am very sorry that at the time I made application that I made such a blunder as to say I would die. I'm now certain that I was foolish at the time, and beg of you, Sir, not to take amis[s] what I wrote. I must state that the authorities are treating us well, sincerely well, no prisoner can complain.

My opinion of this war is that there is only one end, that England *will* reign supreme, and I cannot see why I who have a different opinion from those who still kick rows must remain where I am. I'm convinced that the Boers are struggling for a hopeless case, and since I've come to the conclusion that there can be only one end, I beg of you, Sir, not to send me away, but give me a room, as I wish to remain peacible.

I will now tell you, Sir, my case. I was commandeered and went to the borders of the O.R.C., where I stayed three months. Then we got orders to come to Colesberg. But I got off at Jagersfontein Road and stayed there from the 5th of January 1900 till His Lordship Lord Roberts arrived at Bloemfontein. I was staying with my brother at the time. When the British troops arrived and a week after that I applied for a situation on the railway [*sic*]. I was sent to Bloemfontein for inspection, but was sent back again as I did not take any extra clothing with me. I went to Jagersfontein with a pass I enclosed to you last year, then went back to Bloemfontein the next day, and I was appointed on the railway for number taker, where I worked three, four or five days, I'm not sure. The Provoo Marchel [*sic*] came to me one afternoon and asked where Strydom was. Strydom, Sir, is my brother-in-law and was a Luitenant at the time. I told the P. M. that if Strydom is not shot then he must still be fighting. So he told me that Strydom was in town. I told him that I did not see Strydom. The next morning I was called to the court room. The Provo Marchel was very nice to me, asked me how I was, etz. Then I was sent away to Greenpoint.

Do not think, Sir, that I blame the Authorities atall. They did not know me and of course therefore could not trust me.

Now, Sir, hoping you will take in consideration what my feelings are (I wish to be with civilized people), I remain yours very respectfully, P. J. de Beer.

Notes at the bottom of letter read 'Tent 24' and 'Bermuda, 29.v.1901', which seems to indicate that De Beer was not given 'a room to remain peacible' as requested.

C.J. Bosman was in his own way no less anxious to display his goodwill towards the authorities at Green Point.

Greenpoint Camp No.2, 22.5.01

Col. West, Commandant Prisoners of War

Dear Sir, – As decided by a company of us which I am representing, I beg to inform you about the noises caused the last two evenings by the Uitlanders or foreigners and some of the (our) Boer cowards. In case you want to find out who they are, just send in a body of armed soldiers to corner in those peace disturbers and take them out. We others want quietness, but that will never be as long as these disturbers are going on with their operations.

I have the honour to be, dear Sir, your obedient servant, C.J. Bosman.

P.S. Please don't mention my name, else they'll call me a British subject and bring me into great troubles. I trust you in my P.S. request.

R.G. de Vries was by the evidence of his letter also a Free Stater, and a middle-aged or elderly man. He wrote in some indignation on board the Bavarian *bound for St Helena.*

Bavarian, 19/1/1901

Col. West, *Bavarian*

Dear Sir, – I have the honour to state the following facts which I hope you will kindlij take into consideration.

I am a non-combattant war prisoner, and while five of mij boijs were in the Boor armij I was sent out to Greenpoint on the 3th of April 1900.

When I considered that the country was conquered by Lord Roberts and when I saw the guerilla war commencing I kept a meeting in Camp and I drew up a Memorial and had it signed by p[lus] m[inus] 1200 men. The contents of which I can give you a copij contained that although we had been fighting for our libertij we acknowledged that we were in the power of the English Government and that we had no right to ask to return unless peace was declared, but taking in consideration the ruination of our people in the field we asked to return loijallij to save what could be saved.

In answer to this His Excellencij promised that we should return as soon as hostilities decreased, and that he was verij glad to receive it and would keep [it] in due consideration.

I came to the conclusion that I nor the 1100 [*sic*] men would ever been bannished from South Africa.

I am certain that if Sir Alfred Milner would be informed that I was sent to St Helena he would be dissatisfied, and I trust that you will do what is in your power to let me return.

Mij wife is English and all her relations and we are personallij much interested that England should keep the O.F.S., now the O.R. Colonij, onder its rule to protect the English inhabitants.

In conclusion, some half mad farmers made a row in camp about our memorial and were sent awaij to St Helena on purpose, so you will understand how hard life must be amongst those who were bannished negativelij, I being the cause of it.

Trusting you will kindlij take this in full consideration. Your old servant, R. G. de Vries, Line Captain.

40. 'Jamestown – two Boer prisoners': a snapshot taken by Lawrence Richardson on St Helena in September 1902, some months after the end of the war. It shows tourists proceeding down the middle of the street, the man carrying a box camera, and two of the remaining inhabitants of the prisoner-of-war camp trudging towards the observer to one side, almost unnoticed. (INIL 10355)

No less evocative of this little world is a stray envelope which has survived among the research materials of the late Eric Rosenthal. It is laboriously inscribed 'Mr S.J.P. van Zyl, Prisoner of war Simonstown, Pelles[?], Hospitaal Harlich Castle, C. of Mrs Ds Theron, via Captown', and on the back as 'from his father and mother at Zeekoefontyn distrik Potchefstroom S.A.R., Pos Vereeniging'; the date stamp, which still reads 'Vereeniging Z.A.R.', is for 21 June 1900, in the immediate aftermath of the British occupation of the Transvaal. Given his distinctive initials, Van Zyl had probably been named for President Kruger.

Boer prisoners were despatched variously to St Helena, Bermuda, India or Ceylon, as indicated by passing references in the letters quoted above, and Dominee D.J. Viljoen was among those sent to India. The experiences leading up to his captivity, while not remarkable or even atypical in themselves, are described more fully here in order to illustrate the effects of the war on an average civilian in one of the Republics.

At the outbreak of war Viljoen had been a minister at Reitz in the north-eastern Free State, an area remarkably well covered in the various manuscript records held by the South African Library. In January 1901 the population was summarily evacuated by the British as part of their attempts to stamp out Boer resistance, and Viljoen, finding

41. 'Boer prisoners of war: Sunday morning service in the Dyatalawa Camp, Ceylon'. (Cape Times Weekly, 2.4.1902)

himself designated a 'Class B' prisoner of war, was moved successively to Harrismith, Ladysmith, Durban and Green Point en route to Ceylon. His destination was subsequently changed to India, but he only got as far as Durban, in a batch of 500 prisoners, when the outbreak of bubonic plague caused them to be sent back to Cape Town. It was not until 2 April that they finally embarked on the Roslin Castle *for Bombay.*

The D.J. Viljoen Collection at the South African Library consists of a great deal of material relating to his imprisonment, including what seems to be a first version of his diary and a fuller version compiled and polished for publication, the introduction to the latter (which is quoted here) being dated Bredasdorp, December 1907. He had obviously been taught Dutch well, but he used it self-consciously (he was born at Richmond, Cape Colony), and the polishing was rather over-anxious. [Translation on pp. 152-153.]

Maandag, 22 April [1901]. Wij hadden heden morgen catechesatie. Daarna werd onze bidstond gehouden. Onze hoofdgedachten waren: dankbaarheid dat de Heere ons zoo veilig over de groote wateren geleid had, en gebed dat Hy ons in het vreemde Indië mocht leiden en bewaren. In de namiddag werd de laatste bede van het Onze Vader behandeld.

Dinsdag, 23 April. Toen wy ontwaakten was Bombaai in zicht. Tegen een uur stoomden wy de haven binnen. De hitte was erg. Het getal toeschouwers was zeer groot, en nog grooter zou het geweest zyn als het schip op den volgenden (den bepaalden) dag aangekomen was. De nieuwsgierigheid was toch al te groot om Boeren krygsgevangenen te zien. En toen men ons zag, was men teleurgesteld. Men had zich voorgesteld dat wy korte mannetjes met lange haren en ongekapte baard waren, terwyl de Boer er als alle andere Europeanen uitzag.

Was de nieuwsgierigheid groot, niet minder groot was de belangstelling en de sympathie met ons van meer dan eene zyde. Geen woord van verachting werd er gehoord, en geen teeken van haat en nyd werd er gezien. Hoe verschillend van de Kaapstad, waar onze arme krygsgevangenen in die straten voor alles wat leelyk en bespottelyk is uitgekreten werd.

Daar wy niet toegelaten werden in de stad te gaan, konden wy nu niets van de plaats zien. Tegen 6:20 vertrok de eerste trein met een deel der manschappen en elf officieren. Het overige deel ging met den tweeden trein. Voor ons vertrek zongen de burgers op verzoek van eene Engelsche dame de twee volksliederen. Het was treffend te zien met hoeveel respect het zingen van onze volksliederen door de vele toeschouwers ontvangen werd.

Het was maanlicht, zoodat wy dit toch konden bemerken dat wy door een zeer bergachtig deel gingen. Niet minder dan 26 tunnels gingen wy door. Hoewel in den nacht, waren er by al de stations groote scharen van nieuwsgierigen en belangstellenden. Wy reisden zeer aangenaam, want daar de officieren op parool waren, hadden wy den onmisbaren soldaat by ons niet. Het was dan ook laat in den nacht voordat wy in slaap vielen.

Woensdag, 24 April. Toen wy heden morgen ontwaakten, waren wy erg teleurgesteld. Alles zag er zeer droog uit, daar het lang niet behoorlyk geregend had. Hier en daar zagen wy kleine getallen bokken, op eene plaats een paar wilde bokken. Verder niets anders dan Indianen [sic] met hunne ploegen met twee of vier ossen bespannen, bezig om in de drooge aarde te krabben (ploegen kan men het niet noemen), in de hoop dat de onmisbare regen zou volgen.

Tegen zeven uur in den morgen arriveerden wy aan het station van Ahmednagar. De afstand van het station naar het kamp is zoowat 4 mylen. Wy moesten natuurlyk stappen, en na eene wandeling van zoowat een uur kwamen wy by het fort aan. Toen wy de hooge muren zagen, gevoelden wy ons allesbehalve op ons gemak. Vreemdelingen in een vreemd land, en dan nog in een soort van 'tronk' (gevangenis) opgesloten! Niet minder waren wy treurig gestemd toen wy binnen het fort waren. Alles zag er zeer treurig uit. Byna geen groen blad, de hitte ondragelyk, opgesloten tusschen de hooge muren, en tevens nog doorndraad en de onmisbare gewapenden om ons. De gedachte maakte zich onwillekeurig van ons meester: Hier zullen wy niet lang wezen of een groot aantal zullen hun graf in de vreemde gevonden hebben. Zy het hier vermeld dat het later bleek dat onze vrees ongegrond was, want in al den tyd hebben wy slechts tien gevangenen verloren.

Na onze aankomst werden wy geteld, en toen werd het ontdekt dat een der gevangenen ontsnapt was. Hy heette Grey. Wat van hem geworden is, hebben wy niet kunnen uitvinden. Dit voorval veroorzaakte ons veel ongemak, want wy werden herhaalde malen geteld.

De krygsgevangenen namen hun intrek in bungalos of zink-hutten. Het behoeft nauwelyks vermeld te worden dat wy allen zeer vermoeid waren en dat wy het grootste gedeelte van den dag met slapen doorbrachten.

Viljoen is said to have 'laboured with great success among the burghers, particularly the young men, in the camps at Ahmednagar and Anritzar [Amritsar]'. He arrived back in South Africa in September 1902, to find the village of Reitz largely destroyed and his church and parsonage heavily damaged.

The conditions in the prisoner-of-war camps, while spartan, were not unduly difficult, however, and on the whole there seems to have been a jolly boarding-house spirit among the inmates. The lot of those left behind in South Africa was considerably grimmer, and this applies not only to the men left in the field, but equally and possibly to an even greater extent to the civilians of the two Republics, who were increasingly subjected to restrictions, commandeering, looting, destruction and forced removals.

The prisoner-of-war material collected by Dominee H.C. Hopkins (see p. 76 above) includes letters received by prisoners from their families at home; they seem to form an inter-connected group relating to members of the Uys and Geldenhuys families in the districts of Kroonstad and Heidelberg, Transvaal, and prisoner-of-war camps at Green Point and Ladysmith. B.A. Lourens was, as is clear from his letter, an elderly man, and he had obviously received very little schooling, as was not unusual among members of his generation. [Translation on pp. 153-154.]

Hijdelberg [Tvl.], de 20 Oktober 1900

Lieffe oude broider W.J. Uijs, krijgsgevangge te Groinpund, – U lieffe brief is ons geworde ons [=in?] welstand. Wij bevend ons nog ende uur van genade dog onder veelle liggams iilende en ook de omstandighijs des tijds heef ons ter aarde neergedruk, het leeven is ons bitter. Wij heef nog noid gedag dat wij op ons oude dag en zoo een toistand zou gerak waren wij ons nu bevend. Zij vraaggen waar is uwe God? Lieffe broider, wij heef voor meer dan een jaar geen tijden van eenneg bloidverwand of kenderen, geen letter ontvangen, op u klijnne brieffe aan Uijs heef ik u twee brieven aan u gezonden na Kronstat, nu ontvang wij vier brief-fen tegelijk, een van Jan Iksten, zed bij Nukassel en de tronk, een van Megiel, die is al meer als een mand en Natal op de schip pressenier van oorlog, en nu ontvang ik u brief, mij meldende dat u en lief kenderen te Groinpund ook krijgsgevanne is, en dit is voor ons te veel om te draag voor een oude grijsaard. Broider, wat kan ik tog voor u, kan ik tog niet voor borg staan, dan zal ik u bezorgen als het noidig is. Hoor tog bij de overhijd. U oude zuster is ik jammer voor.

Ons leeven gaat voorbij met zugten en gebeeden, daar is veelle van ons dierbarre heengegaan zooals de broider Hans Uijs, Waterkloof, en C. Uijs, Maskloof, en nog veellen anderen. Hoi gad het met lieffrou Zesara toin zij van huis weg is? Hoe gaat het met u gezondheijd en de kamp? Lief Pie[t?] Geldenhuis? Zeg an hem ik begeer een brief van hem.

Wij groiet al u kenderen en u zelf met een kus der liefte. De Heer zij u en de uwe nabij, doi zijn anschijn over u legten, hij zij u genadig, hij doid zijn anschijn over u ligten, hij zij u genadig, is de beede van u de broider en zuster, B.A. en A.W. Lourens.

P.S. Kette en Ben is op het oogenblik hier aangekoomen en Vranses is ook met haar kar hier. U liefte zuster vraag of zij niet voor u een Bijbel kan stuur. Als [ik] wes dat ons govermend mijn zou toilaat u en de andere te zien, zou [ik] kom. Arme Giel vraag mijn geld, mar ik weet niet hoi ik het bij hem zal krij.

Judging by the contents of her letter F. Geldenhuys was a relatively young woman with a small child. Her Dutch, though far from faultless, was much more fluent and self-confident than that of Lourens, although she was clearly not a prolific letterwriter and expressed herself largely in the set expressions she would have been taught at school. She was writing to her husband in Green Point; from other letters in the collection it appears that Honingspruit was in the Kroonstad district of the Free State. The references to her own situation are not clear, but she seems to have been experiencing difficulty in looking after her mother or mother-in-law. The multiple references to relatives and friends in captivity all over South Africa and beyond are typical of this prisoner-of-war correspondence. [Translation on p. 154.]

Honengspruit, 25ste Maart 1901

Waarde en lieve man, – Met blydschap heef ik u brief van de 12de Maart ontvangen waaren gy my een wynig geld vraag. De goede vriend van ons het voor u vyf pond gezonden. Ik hoop dat gy het al ontvangen heef.

Met ons gaat het zeer goed, wy klaag over niets, alles volop. Het reegen hier mooi, byna elken dag. Henni is slim en praat, alle[e?]n vol platjes streeke. Ik moet veel met Ma sukel, is swaar en ongemakkelyk.

Gy seg ik moet al weeke aan u schryf. Ik het een pyn en myn regter arm en de gebeef is en myn arm zoo erg dat het voor my zeer henderlyk is om te schryf. Dit alles ontstaan door de swaare ligchaam wat ik moet regeer. Ik zal doen wat ik kan.

Met de ander vamielie gaat het goed. Geef myn beste groete aan al de bekende, ook aan broeder Frederik. Schryf my waar hy is. Geef myn groete aan Papa en aan al de

42. 'The Du Buisson family abuse Colonel Firman', an incident photographed by R.B. Pott in the Senekal district on 31 December 1900, and explained more fully in the text. Two of the women are wearing traditional frilled sun-bonnets, while two others have improvised a form of headscarf. (INIL 10140)

broeders als gy weer aan hun schryf. Ik heef de laatste February aan u een brief geschryf.
   Noeme my u vrouw, groete u met een kus der liefde, F. Geldenhuis.

The systematic destruction of farm buildings and supplies which had begun in the winter of 1900 affected all the civilians who had stayed behind when the men had gone to war: white women, children and old people, and all blacks. At first the occupants of the devastated farms seem to have been left to fend for themselves, as appears from an incident in the Senekal district described by R.B. Pott in the diary entry below; brief though it is, it conveys something of the militant spirit which marked Boer womenfolk in general, and it is made all the more interesting by being accompanied by a snapshot of the Du Buisson women parleying with the British.

Monday, 31st December 1900. Marched at 6 a.m. and occupied Tafelberg, where we tried to get helio communication with Winburg. This was found impossible, so we

43. 'House burning'. A snapshot with a laconic description from the album of R.B. Pott, who was stationed in the north-eastern Free State over the period 1900-1901; it accompanies diary entries for September 1900. (INIL 10058)

visited the farm of De Buisson, where we found no less than six women or girls concealed in the mountains. A great scene ensued, and the Colonel decided to take them in to Senekal. Their clothes were taken out of the caves in the mountain side. Eventually the Colonel decided (I cannot but think wrongly) to leave them, so we took what we wanted and left them.

As an example of how the women endeavoured to keep the men fighting, one of the daughters gave a Kaffir the following letter to give to the Boers: 'Dear Brother, the English have taken us, so now you must fight, not only for your country, but for me, fight to the end and God will preserve you.'

We returned to Senekal about 3 p.m., not having fired a shot. Page went in the hospital today with enteric.

Many women survived on the veld in a semi-independent state for a surprisingly long time, accompanied by their families, servants and cattle, as is shown in the reminiscence quoted below. It is part of a brief manuscript of which the South African Library holds only a photocopy of unknown provenance.

The writer of this short account appears from internal evidence to have been living at

Glen Alphen in the Bethlehem district of the Free State, and a subsequent note on the original identifies her as Aletta Sophy Schabort, née Bester, who was thirty years old at the time. She formed part of a group of three women with their families; the menfolk referred to were obviously still on commando and must have come to help them guard their cattle. They were threatened by British units operating from Standerton in the Transvaal, where B.J. Jones was at this time stationed (see pp. 104-106 below), and must have been moving about the Vrede district, as she specifically mentioned De Langesdrift on the Klip River. At this time the guerrilla forces under De Wet were active in this area, which explains the large-scale military activity on the part of the British. Her Dutch is faulty but fluent, and one has the impression of a living voice rather than a written record, of someone talking rather than writing. [Translation on pp. 154-156.]

Op Donderdag, 7 November [1901] moest wy afscheid van ons dierbaarens nemen die toen weder veiligheid voor hun vee moesten zoeken. Wy echter, tante Corneilja Buys en kinderen, Martje Boshoff en ik met mij kinderen en een klein kafvertje, bleven toen op de plaats van Magiel Uijs, Kalverspruyt, waar ons verteld was dat ons beschaafde vijand geen vrouwen en kinderen meer vangen.

Toen kwam er een kamp van Standerton, die trek toen naby ons voorby en kampeer omtrent 1/2 uur te paard van ons, hun spioene kwam tot naby ons en draai daar weer om. De kamp bleef op lager plaats agter Tafelkop twee of drie dagen. Ag, wy hadden bittere daagen, geen nacht of dag hadden wy rust, daar wy altyd de vyand iedere ogenblikt verwachten, en wy weten niets is voor hen te goed. Wy spion behoorlyk by beurten op een rantje vlak achter de woning.

Op laats kwam de blyde tyding, de vyand is vertrokken in richting Frankfort. Ag hoe blyde waaren wy toen om te denken dat wy zonder die bittere vlucht vry gekoomen ben, want de eerste man die er kwam, Frans v.d. Berg, geef ons verzekering dat ze allen Wilger[ri]vier door ben, en dat er tien kampen en de richting was. Ag hoe zwaar gevoelde wy ons toen weder op nieuw over ons mans en vee die wy niet weten wat van hun geworden is, maar op laats dacht wy, als de Lieve Heer ons mannen en kinderen maar vry door helpen, al bleven de vee en de slagt.

Nu zit wy met angstige harten te wachten naar tyding van ons dierbaaren. Op laats kwam T.B. er aan op de 13 November laat, met of na zon onder, wy erken dadelyk de paarden op heelen afstand, maar wy gevoelden zeer sleg, daar wy wisten dat de een en myn kar getrokken heeft en wy dachten alles is in de slag gebleven, maar toen moesten wy allen hooren hoe bitter dat zij door die kampen gekoomen ben en karren alles en steek moes laaten, niet wisten wat er van geworden was, ook niet westen wat de morgen met ons menschen gebeuren was na T.B. van hun weg is, want hy was schaars weg toen was er een kamp op dezelfde plek, zoo ik dink de Langens Drift. Ja, wy gevoelen diep de lot van ons dierbares, maar wat staat ons te wachten?

De kamp staat toen omtrent een of meer uuren van ons by Albertus van Wyk, naby Leeuwkop, maar recht in de richting naar ons. Wy hadden een bittere

44. 'Frankfort parsonage', a snapshot of one of the many Free State villages destroyed by the British in the course of the scorched earth policy, taken by Lawrence Richardson in November 1902: 'the sight of it came as a shock,' he wrote concerning the ruined village. (INIL 10513)

nacht, [ik] kon niet tot rusten koomen al voor ik myn lot niet met God inge-worpen heef. Laat koomen wat wil, ik ben onder Gods hand en besturing.

T.B. was de avond van ons weg om veiligheid voor hem en myn twee koeijen te zoekken die toen onder zorg van de kafvertjie en richten gezonden word tot hy by hem zou koomen om te zeggen welke richting. Zeer bekommert was ik dien nacht over T.B., dat hy meschien zeer moeg ben en hem morgen verslaap, enstede vroeg te spioen voor hem en koeijen welke richting te gaan.

De ander dag was wy zeer vroeg half donker uit bed om te zien wat de plaan van de Draake was, en dan ook al ons klere so veel wy konden op elkander aan te trekken, daar hy, die Draake, de gewoonte had alles te verbranden, en u dan net met kleren aan u lyf te laaten zonder kos of klere of bedegoed.

Wy zag hen toen koomen met groote angs wat zal van ons worden, kamp en alles kwam op ons af, eigenlyk kwam de eerste klomp, was rechte onvriendelyk, want wy hooren hen goed dood schoten, het moet en hond of en kalf gewees zyn. Wy houden ons als wy hen niet verstanden, om uit te vinden wat gaande was. Er was toen een ou jong die zegt, Julle moet klaar maak, die kamp zal julle zeker weg vat, wy heeft al en heele klomp vrouwens; maar toen was wy diep geslagen om te dink dat ons scheiding meschien voor eeuwig was en wy het niet gedacht

89

heeft, maar wy dachten wy zou nog los koomen door de gebreklyk zoon van 14 jaar van Stofvel Botha.

Nou kwam de twede klomp onder Allison. Net toen hy my zacht zegt hy, U man heeft laaste nacht kom *serunder*. Ik zegt toen, Ik heb zoo en lafhart van een man niet. Toen vraag hy, Is u dan niet Mrs T.B.? Ik zeg, Nee. [Toen staat ons ou maat M. daar binnen en de kamer te lachten wat makeer T. dink hy heeft my er nooit niets van gezegt, dink daar alles zeker afgesproke werk was, want hulle was dien middag byna altyd alleen.][1] Toen ik zoo ver Allison zeg, Nou ja, maak haastig klaar, T.B. zegt jullie moet kom. Nee, wy wil niet kom, en ziet die arme gebreklek kind. Haastig was die dokter by, maar geen genade, ons moest haastig maak, de wagen kom. Toen word al de goed die wy geborgen had zoo lang op gespoor door die vuile handsuppers en gewapende kafvers, die veele zyn. Ja, alles breek en verniel zy in neem zoo veel zy kan weg voor hun arme kaal vamilies.

Aletta Schabort and her family were taken to a so-called refugee camp at Standerton and subsequently to one at Merebank in Natal, where they were to remain until the end of the war. Her husband was captured by the British a few months afterwards and sent to India.

As farm burning, the destruction of crops and the denudation of the countryside became part of Kitchener's official strategy, all civilians came to be swept away, usually much against their will, and provision had to be made for them. By the end of 1900 there was already no more accommodation for refugees in Pretoria, and this must have been the reason for the establishment of a camp in the suburb of Arcadia to the east of the town the following winter. It does not appear in any of the official accounts which have been traced, and possibly had an informal status, the camp at Irene to the south of the town being the major camp in the area. It is recalled here because Johanna Lorentz (see p. 52 above) visited the inmates and left a graphic account of her visits.

There were eventually to be more than forty refugee or concentration camps for whites spread all over South Africa, and a further number for blacks, which are not nearly as well documented. They had been improvised under the difficult conditions of wartime and their administration was in the hands of military men unacquainted with the needs of women and children. Initially at any rate conditions there were poor and there was a high death rate – the figure of 26 370 white women and children is recorded on the Women's Memorial at Bloemfontein – and the memory of this traumatic experience was to be a source of bitterness for several generations. In the camps for blacks, conditions were considerably worse, and many more people must have died than the 14 154 (one in ten) whose deaths were recorded in the official statistics.

On 17 July it had been proclaimed that 'The wives, children or relatives residing in the town and district of Pretoria of Burghers in arms' would, unless able to support themselves, be deported 'to a place or places beyond the British lines', as reported here

---

1. Passage placed between square brackets thus in the original; punctuation and intended meaning unclear.

45. 'Pietersburg refugees en route to Pretoria', from a newspaper photograph. Pietersburg in the Northern Transvaal was not captured by the British until 8 April 1901, after which, according to the official history of the war, 'Boer inhabitants were sent back in large batches to Pretoria'. (Cape Times Weekly, 22.5.1901)

by Miss Lorentz, but this threat was never carried out. [Translation on pp. 156-158.]

23 Juli [1901]. Heden morgen bezocht ik op nieuw het vrouwenkamp op Arcadia. Vele tenten waren leeg, en mij werd medegedeeld dat een groot aantal vrouwen op nieuw naar Irene was vervoerd.

In eene tent die ik binnenging, vond ik een meisje van 11 jaar ziek aan long-ontsteking. Zij scheen mij bijna stervende. De moeder, Mrs Coetzee, vertelde mij dat zij onlangs van Schurftbergen waren binnengebracht, dat het kind al maanden lang over pijn op de borst had geklaagd, dat zij op reis naar hier drie nachten onder de open lucht hadden moeten slapen, terwijl het 's nachts vinnig koud was en vroor, en dat het kind toen kou had gevat. Zij lag nu al een week ziek. Dr Van Wijk was voor drie dagen bij haar geroepen en had haar medicijnen gegeven, die de moeder echter niet meer ingaf omdat het kind er erg benauwd door was geworden. Daar lag zij nu ijlende, en niemand wist wat te doen. De moeder zat maar in stille wanhoop met droge oogen gade te slaan.

Ik ging de stad in en mocht toevallig den dokter treffen in zijne apotheek. Hij was dadelijk bereid naar het kamp te gaan en tenminste goeden raad te geven aangaande de verdere behandeling indien de moeder bleef weigeren de medicijnen in te geven.

46. 'Kaffir kraal for refugee Natives, Elandsfontein'; one of a series of snapshots from an album apparently belonging to a nurse attached to the Imperial Yeomanry Hospital at Elandsfontein (now Germiston). (INIL 2862)

Zooeven hoor ik dat het arme kind overleden is, en ook dat de familieleden van den President die nog in Pretoria waren is aangezegd dat zij het land moeten verlaten. Er werd vandaag ook verteld dat het militaire bestuur voornemens is al de vrouwen der nog op kommando zijnde mannen over de grenzen te zetten.

25 Juli. Heden morgen bezocht ik opnieuw het vrouwenkamp om Mrs Kleynhans, die drie kinderen ziek heeft aan de mazelen, lakens en Bovril te brengen. Zij lagen alle drie op een kist waarover een paar dekens gespreid waren. Ik gaf haar den raad de kinderen met lauw water af te wasschen, daar zij geheel zwart waren van stof en vuil.

Ik begaf mij daarop naar de tent van Mrs Coetzee, de vrouw wier dochter eergisteren stierf. De begrafenis had nog niet plaats gehad, omdat de dokter wegens drukke bezigheden zijn certificaat van het overlijden nog niet had ingezonden. Terwijl ik met de vrouw stond te praten aan den ingang harer tent zeide zij plotseling: 'Daar komt het lijkwagentje aan.' De arme vrouw had ternauwernood tijd om te beseffen wat dit voor haar inhad. Een klein kind huilde onophoudelijk en moest geholpen worden, Twee andere kinderen, een meisje van 13 en een jongen van 7, lagen ziek te bed. Een jongen van 14 had nieuwe kleeren aan en een rouwband om zijn hoed, en zou de eenige volger achter het lijkje zijn.

De lijkwagen kwam vóór de tent, en onmiddellijk verzamelden zich verscheidene Boeren, vrouwen en kinderen vóór den ingang. Een oudere man verzocht ons

47. 'Another native concentration camp: Krugersdorp. The coloured refugees in the photograph are awaiting the distribution of the daily ration.' (From, H.W. Wilson: After Pretoria; volume 2)

te zingen Ps. 103:8, 'Gelijk het gras is ons kortstondig leven,/ Gelijk een bloem die op het veld verheven,' enz., enz. Eerst was er niemand die kon inzetten, maar eindelijk begon een jonge Boerenvrouw, geholpen door eene vriendin, op krijschenden, slependen toon te zingen, waarop wij allen invielen.

Het was een bonte menigte van mannen, vrouwen en kleine kinderen, meest allen op echt Boerenwijze gekleed, en van de meest verschillende leeftijden. Tegenover mij stond een oude man met een rooden zakdoek die met een punt op zijn rug viel om den hals, gebogen, en het haar op echte Hugenotenmanier van de kruin naar alle zijden vallende, en die mij verplaatste met mijn gedachten in den tijd der hagepreeken. Over hem heen rustte mijn blik op de rivier en op den Magaliesberg in de blauwe verte.

Toen wij het vers hadden uitgezongen, deed de voorganger een gebed. Hij dankte God dat waar de bode des doods in ons midden was verschenen, wij de overledene in hare laatste rustplaats konden wegbergen, terwijl zooveel vrienden en betrekkingen in deze tijden de eeuwigheid ingingen zonder dat hunne naaste betrekkingen wisten waar zij rustten. Hij dankte er ook voor dat wij door dit sterven werden herinnerd aan onzen eigen dood, die aanstaande was. Hij bad voor de moeder die haar kind had moeten afgeven, maar voor wie het een troost was te weten dat haar dochtertje was heengegaan tot Hem die gezegd heeft: 'Laat de kinderkens tot Mij komen, want derzulken is het koninkrijk der hemelen', enz.

Toen het gebed geëindigd was, deelde hij mede dat de autoriteiten slechts *tien* minuten toestonden voor de lijkdienst; hij kon dus niet uit den Bijbel voorlezen noch een toespraak houden. Hij zeide alleen nog dat al had men elkander zoo lief, zoo lief dat men niet van elkander kon scheiden, dat al drukte de moeder haar kind aan het hart en wilde het niet loslaten, als de dood kwam, moest zij het alleen laten gaan, daarheen vergezelde ons niemand. Hij verzocht toen weer te zingen Gez. 10:8 en 9, 'Als wij de doodsvallei betreên, / Laat ons elk aardsche vriend alleen,' enz. En, 'Komt, treên wij dan gemoedigd voort,' enz. Vervolgens zeide hij nog tot de moeder dat zij met David zeggen kon, 'Zij zal niet wederkeeren tot mij, maar ik zal tot haar gaan.'

Daarop namen eenige jonge mannen het kistje op, plaatsten het in den lijkwagen, en een ieder ging weer zijns weegs. Langzaam daalde de wagen den heuvel af naar de rivier, door slechts één gevolgd, het veertienjarig broertje van het gestorven meisje.

Jacoba Lorentz returned to Europe shortly afterwards, where she is known to have lectured in Switzerland on conditions in the camps .

There is a good deal of material on the concentration camps, and on the war in general, among the papers of Johanna Lorentz, who observed accurately and wrote well, and she was the author of another perceptive and evocative account of the occupied Transvaal capital in wartime. It describes the funeral of the aged Mrs Gezina Kruger, the wife of the President, who had been obliged to stay behind when her husband left the town before the approach of the British, and who died in her home in Pretoria on 20 July 1901.

The house described is the present Kruger House in Church Street West, and the funeral service in the Gereformeerde Kerk opposite was conducted by Dominee H.S. Bosman of the N.G. or H. Kerk, the only Afrikaans minister remaining in the occupied town. [Translation on pp. 158-159.]

22 Juli [1901]. Eergister stierf Mrs Kruger, vrouw van den President. Zij was meestal lijdende, en was zoo gezet dat zij nooit liep, maar de kleinste afstanden per rijtuig moest afleggen. Reeds sedert jaren liet zij zich elken Zondag naar de kerk rijden, die tegenover haar huis aan de overzijde der straat staat. In den laatsten tijd ging zij zeer gebukt onder al de ellende die de oorlog voor land en volk bracht, en ook in hare eigene familie ondervond zij veel verdriet: de President nu reeds een jaar weg, een zoon en zijne vrouw leven slecht, en verscheidene harer naaste familieleden sneuvelden of kwamen om tengevolge van den oorlog, ook een paar harer kinderen en kleinkinderen. Zij was een eenvoudig, vriendelijk mensch, een echte Christin, die zich temidden van al het wereldsche dat haar omringde zooveel mogelijk trouw bleef aan de ouderwetsche boerenmanier van leven, en die dan ook standvastig weigerde den Goeverneur of een der hooggeplaatste Engelsche officieren te ontmoeten, zeggende dat zij maar een eenvoudige vrouw was en met zulke menschen niet wist om te gaan. Zij werd vergood door

48. 'The funeral of Mrs Kruger: the cortege leaving her late residence in Church Street West for the cemetery. The building seen on the right background is the new Dopper Church, where the Ex-President was wont to preach.' The photograph is by B. Alter, Pretoria. (Cape Times Weekly, 7.8.1901)

hare kinderen en kleinkinderen, plus-minus tachtig in getal.

Verleden week kreeg zij eene longontsteking, zoo als in deze tijd van 't jaar, waarin 't stof duimen dik op den grond ligt, veel voorkomt, maar de eigenlijke oorzaak van haar dood was zwakte van het hart. Het is een groot verlies voor den President, maar voor haar is het een uitkomst, zij trok zich de dingen erg aan en was daar niet tegen bestand.

Gister (Zondag) middag om drie uur had de begrafenis plaats. Ik ging er met eene mijner kennissen heen. Het rijtuig moest op vrij groote afstand van het huis stilstaan. De straat was zwart van menschen en rijtuigen. Het gedrang was erg, en wij konden er slechts met moeite in slagen het huis binnen te gaan, over-al wemelde het van menschen. Wij gingen eene groote kamer binnen en vonden daar de kist staan, bedekt met kransen en bewaakt door eenige Boeren. De kist was van gepolijst eikehout; op een metalen plaat stond haar naam en leeftijd, 67 jaar, en kransen bedekten de kist en de vloer eromheen. De familieleden zagen wij niet.

Wij begaven ons daarop naar eene andere groote kamer aan de overzijde van de gang. In den versten hoek zat eene vrouw in het zwart te huilen. Afgaande op haar uiterlijk begreep ik dat zij eene der dochters van den President was. Tegenover haar

95

zaten twee vrouwen in de gewone Boerendracht met kapjes op en een derde met gewone kleding, alle drie echter in het zwart. De vrouw met den hoed op en de voile voor zat met harde stem teksten uit den Bijbel aan te halen en de huilende vrouw op te wekken tot berusting. 't Maakte een eigenaardige indruk, en deed mij denken aan den ouden tijd toen er menschen in de kolonie waren die den titel droegen van Ziekentrooster.

Het gewoel en gewemel van menschen, de groote kamer, waarin een levensgroot portret van den President hing en waarin op een afstand nog een Boerenvrouw zat, ook met een kapje op, en een andere in de tegenwoordige kleederdracht, de droefheid van de vrouw die huilde en op niets acht sloeg, maar scheen te luisteren naar de vrouw die sprak, de beide andere zwijgende, zwarte figuren, half met de rug naar mij toegekeerd – ik zal den indruk die dit alles op mij maakte niet licht vergeten.

Toen wij de familieleden die wij zochten niet vonden, begaven wij ons weer naar buiten en in het gedrang, en slaagden er met veel moeite in de kerk aan de overzijde der straat te bereiken, waar een lijkdienst zou gehouden worden. De kerk was stampvol. Toen wij zagen dat er geen kans was binnen te komen, gingen wij naar de consistoriekamer, waar nog overvloed van ruimte was. Ik deed de deur open om de preek te kunnen volgen, en werd door iemand die opstond een stoel aangeboden. Ds. Bosman las een hoofdstuk uit de Openbaring, en vervolgens nam hij uit Richteren tot tekste 'Eene Moeder in Israël'. Hij sprak met veel gevoel en op eenvoudige wijze over hare verdienste als moeder voor hare kinderen, als moeder voor haar volk en als Christin, vooral er den nadruk op leggende dat zij een oprechte, eenvoudige, innig vrome Christin was geweest en een stille in den lande, van wie nochtans grooten invloed was uitgegaan. Tot besluit liet hij zingen uit Psalm 25, 'Zie op mij in gunst van boven', het 'mij' echter telkens veranderende in 'hem', en het alzoo toepassende op den President. Het was zeer aandoenlijk hem te hooren lezen, 'Eenzaam is hij en verschoven./ Ja d'ellende drukt hem neer,' enz.

Daarop begaf de stoet zich naar het kerkhof, waarheen een groot deel van het publiek hem volgde. En zoo is zij dan niet meer, die sedert het vertrek van de President de gemeenschappelijke band was tusschen het volk onderling. Een gevoel van leegte overmeestert ons waar wij denken aan de ledige plaats, het ledige huis, zoo lange tijd het middelpunt waarom velen die anders uit elkaar zouden zijn gegaan zich vereenigden.

In a sense the death and funeral of Gezina Kruger symbolised the end of the old Republican Transvaal and all it had stood for. Three years later the aged President died in exile in Switzerland, and on 16 December 1904 he was laid to rest beside her.

49. (opposite). 'The convoy leaving camp', a snapshot from the album of R.B. Pott, taken in the Harrismith district in November 1900 (detail). It illustrates in a striking way the scale of British military operations in South Africa, which besides troops involved large numbers of Black scouts, drivers and labourers, as well as many thousands of horses, mules and oxen. (INIL 10093)

THE VICTORS
(1901)

However secure the British may have felt about the outcome of the war when Roberts left South Africa in December 1900, their victory, such as it was, was hollow, and consisted of little more than a precarious hold on the towns and villages. While they might have looked on themselves as victors, the use of the term in the heading to this chapter is in fact ironic, as will be clear from the accounts quoted here.

By early 1901, J.B. Jardine found himself in the south-eastern Transvaal, flushing out roving Boer commandoes on the border of Swaziland, with some help, as he himself admits, from the Swazi, 'white man's war' or not. His account of playing polo, feasting on peaches and bayonetting sheep amid constant rain and continual sniping has an oddly dreamlike if not surrealistic quality.

The losses at Bothwell which Jardine mentions relate to an attack by the commando of Louis Botha on 6 February. 'K. of K.' is the Commander-in-Chief, Lord Kitchener of Khartoum: the peace negotiations with Botha in which he was involved proved to be abortive, and the 'rebel question' refers to the position of the Cape Colonists who were fighting with the Boers. 'Nullahs' (an Anglo-Indian term) are gullies or river beds, and 'being Stellenbosched', an expression which originated during the war, is defined by Charles Pettman in his book Africanderisms *as 'To be relegated, as the result of incompetence, to a position in which little harm can be done.' The 'Majuba business' was, of course, the Anglo-Transvaal War of 1880-1881.*

Burntop, Swazi border, 2nd March 1901

Dearest Mother, – I think I wrote from Lake Chrissie last; I wonder if you ever got the letter. Since then I have had no opportunity of writing, and as a matter of fact I have none now, but sooner or later we will be able to send letters to the line via Piet Retief.

What with our losses at Bothwell, horse sickness and exhaustion – the latter chiefly due to shortage of forage – we can only mount 90 men now. The mounted troops, i.e. Imperial Light Horse, Mounted Infantry and ourselves, started from Wonderfontein about 1100 strong; now only 650 are mounted.

However, some useful work has been done in the way of capturing Boeren and their possessions and destroying what we have been unable to take along.

The Boers in this part of the country and their families had not felt the draw-

50. 'British troops, Victoria West', from the album of the MacRobert family of the farm Wagenaarskraal. (Photo 1982-75)

backs of war until we came, but they are doing so now, and it has been fatal to them their retiring into Swazi Land.

News came officially last night about K. of K.'s meeting at Middleburg with Louis Botha at the initiative of the latter (an important point), but I have not much faith in much resulting from it. The rebel question will be the difficulty. It is impossible for K. of K. to let them off, and Botha cannot very well desert his friends who have lost so much in helping the Transvaal.

Owing to the swollen state of the rivers we have had no groceries since the 18th ultimo until yesterday, when seven waggons brought in two days' supplies from Piet Retief. Of course Mess supplies have nearly run out and there is a scarcity of tobacco everywhere. Being the most remote of the columns, our chances of restocking are very small before the column gets back again. It is rather hard luck, as they only warned us for three weeks of it. I am using my last cake of soap.

At the present moment as far as we know for certain Knox (18th Hussars) has a brigade at Piet Retief and Alderson is there too with Mounted Infantry. Campbell is in front of us somewhere on the Swazi border, and Allenby with a small force is somewhere east of Piet Retief at the Police Drift.

51. 'View of Vryburg: Somerset Light Infantry passing through the town', a photograph taken by Townshend & Co. (Cape Times Weekly, 24.4.1901)

I believe we are to stick pretty close to the Swazi border most of the trek and in Swazi Land. Swazi Land, as you may imagine, is a villainous country of nullahs, rocks and ravines to move in, but this should be greatly neutralized by our using our friends the Swazis as scouts.

Colonel Henry has at this moment most of the mounted troops with him 12 miles off in Swazi Land, and they have just made a good haul of 1200 oxen, 24 waggons and 56 Boers, also many sheep. They should be back to-day.

Three of the chief men of the Swazis arrived here the day before yesterday to get their final instructions from Smith Dorrien, and seemed very pleased. As a result they commenced yesterday by looting several Boer farms round here, one or two of which contained women who, however, are now being brought into camp prior to be[ing] despatched to the line. We have sent away a great many since this trek began, and I think it is already having a great effect.

9th Feb. We marched 10 miles to Lillieburn over very open country when we were confronted by a deep and swollen stream, so we encamped on the near side. The Imperial Light Horse and our two squadrons had in the moving pressed on after a Boer convoy 5 miles beyond the drift and did not get back until dark.

McKenzie who commands the Imperial Light Horse is the man who used to play polo very often against us for Dargle and is a born cavalry leader. I wish I had more like him. With our two squadrons supporting and guarding the flank he galloped past waggon after waggon, turning them back one by one until he reached the end of them. Horses were so beat that he had only about 10 men with him when he reached the last waggon. Four field guns crossed the drift with great difficulty, disappearing altogether under the water, and covered the retirement to Lillieburn. I don't know the number of the cattle and sheep, but it ran to thousands, 80 waggons and 30 Cape carts, 2 Boeren killed and a few prisoners.

10th Feb. The Umpeluzi was still so swollen that it took all day to cross it and build a bridge, so we camped 3 miles on at Warberton.

11th Feb. After a few hours spent in sheep slaughter with bayonets, we marched to Craigie Lea when we were stopped by the Umpeluzi again. The killing was most necessary, though beastly, as sheep delay a march frightfully and we had far too many for even a force of our size to look after.

In the evening some Imperial Light Horse and a squadron of ours crossed a drift – a real bad one – and captured 20 Boer waggons four miles on. Campbell was seven miles on our right all day.

12th Feb. By the bye, there was a lot of sniping yesterday and we had 2 men in A squadron wounded.

This day we spent in crossing by a bridge. Several mules were drowned, and one man I believe. Another Boer convoy was nearly taken to the north-east, but it got among some awful rocky country along the Swazi border, and being well guarded, our people 'reneged' wisely. Camped close to Busby on the south bank. Sniping in the afternoon.

This district is called New Scotland, and is owned by a Scotsman called McCorquodale whose father came out before the Majuba business and brought a lot of emigrants with him from Scotland. The Boers have swindled him out of a lot of it, but he still has 600 000 acres, and it is good grazing land. Busby is 6000 acres and the rental is £27.10.0. This is one of the few Scotch families left, as most went after Majuba. They know very little about the war, and evidently live a very quiet existence.

13th Feb. Marched at 4.30 a.m. to Maryvale and camped on the south bank of Umtuli. Sniping now and then.

14th Feb. Marched to Amsterdam, describing a semi-circle to the east into Swazi Land. Left a post of Mounted Infantry and Infantry at Miller's Store, where there was a lot of sniping. Got in late. Campbell's column got in also early in the day. I have a sort of idea that I have written to you already about Amsterdam, but am not sure; I think I must have written to you since Lake Chrissie.

15th and 16th Feb. Rained like poison.

17th Feb. I formed to-day with 20 men part of the escort to about 80 waggons containing Boer families from Amsterdam and vicinity and empty supply waggons towards Piet Retief as far as Wolnenkop [*sic*]. I dined there with the 18th Hussars. Fiendish rain of night, and did not get to sleep until 11.30.

18th Feb. Saw convoy well on its way and taken over by some of Alderson's Mounted Infantry, and then returned to Amsterdam. Awful outing.

19th Feb. Poured all day. Camp a marsh.

20th Feb. Imperial Light Horse captured numerous stock on Swazi border, as did also the Mounted Infantry. Rain.

21st Feb. Rained all day and night. The two posts on Swazi border came back to Amsterdam.

22nd to 24th Feb. Rained more or less day and night.

25th Feb. Marched 3 1/2 miles to Compies River. Too full to cross.

26th Feb. Marched across river as far as Wolnenkop. A little sniping. Had a good feed of peaches at a farm and secured some for the Mess.

27th Feb. Marched 12 miles as far as Burntop. Had to make a circuit to the left, as the direct road was too marshy. Crossed Shela River and passed Alderson's force, camped to the south of it. Five Boers surrendered.

28th Feb. Halted at Burntop close to Schwabe's Store, which is in Swazi Land. Reconnoitered with King, Dugdale and Fanshawe (19th Hussars) beyond mission station for supplies for Mess in the afternoon. We got ten hens and chickens, and saw no Boers. Henry took out small force with pom-pom in the morning into Swazi Land to intercept Boer convoy, which turned north. Fine weather lately. Swazi Chiefs came in to interview Smith Dorrien.

1st March. The force detached into Swazi Land has secured their prey as mentioned above. We have a lot of Boer waggons and stock marked down between the Assegai and Compies Rivers in Swazi Land. Allenby is guarding the drifts of the former, and we are to squash them up against him.

2nd March. I spent a very wet night at outposts last night, and on reaching the men at 5.30 a.m. some Mauser bullets rattled over the tarpaulin. The sniping party, however, made off at once.

3rd March. King took out a small force this morning to destroy a mill and bring away the flour. We heard his guns going during lunch time, and when he got back in the evening it appeared that we had 2 men wounded and the 19th also 2 wounded. The sniping occurred as soon as they began to leave the mill.

4th March. Dugdale (18th Hussars), brother of ours, came in from Piet Retief a few minutes ago and says that they have just unearthed 3 Boer guns at that place. Pulteney's column and Knox' are there at present, while Dartnell's is at Luneburg. No word up to date of K. of K. and Botha. French is optimistic about it.

Any amount of Boer families came in last night – a very low class, those in this part of the country. Burn-Murdoch (Royals) is to be Stellenbosched, I hear. French was annoyed at his bringing his convoy from Newcastle to Luneburg so slowly. The latter's wire to K. of K. on the subject, pitching into the former, had to pass through the former's signalling station too. Very funny!

There is an outward mail to-morrow morning, so I will try to get this off by it. To-day is a lovely one, a regular cold weather day; I hope this will continue. I think we will move on Piet Retief about the 8th, and doubt if we will go any further south.

It is very annoying getting no mails, and perhaps we may have two more months

52. 'Lieuts Mentz, Barrett & Knott, Lieut. Lambley, Major Downes, Lieut. Elliott, Capt. Chrisp, Dr. Williams, portion of garrison, Petrusville', a snapshot from the Barrett Albums; the names given in the caption identify the men from the back row to the front and from the left to the right in each row. The house is decorated with fine fretwork, and there a comfortable armchair on the veranda. (INIL 2797)

of this trek. The Swazis up to date have not done much to help us, but they are A1 at herding stock, which they take toll of on every available opportunity. They should prove useful as scouts. They seem to have very few rifles, and they undoubtedly funk the Boers. Were they Basutos it would be a very different matter.

I will close now. I wonder when I will get a letter from you next. We hear nothing of what is going on in Cape Colony.

Hoping all are fit, and best love from your ever affectionate son, J.B. Jardine. 5th March '01.

Jardine and his colleagues were, of course, engaged in much the same operations as the British units stationed at Standerton, a little to the west of them, by whom Aletta Schabort and her companions were captured (see pp. 88-90 above). B.J. Jones was actually stationed in the Standerton area, and in his account of operations there he refers to De Langesdrift on the Klip River which is mentioned by Mrs Schabort; his description of his men 'treasure hunting' for personal possessions hidden on the farm they had just burned down

53. 'Lieut.-General Sir H.M.L. Rundle, K.C.B., C.M.G., D.S.O., commanding 8th Division; Photo by Elliott & Fry', whose aimless activities in the Eastern Free State were described by J.B. Jones in his diary entries as 'rundling'. (From, The Times History of the War in South Africa, IV)

is also reminiscent of her account: 'Toen word al de goed die wy geborgen had zoo lang op gespoor door die vuile handsuppers en gewapende kafvers.'

The verb 'Stellenbosch' has been explained in the introduction to Jardine's letter above. Lieut.-Genl. Leslie Rundle, who was in command of the British forces in the eastern Free State, has already been glimpsed in happier days during the surrender of Prinsloo in the Brandwater Basin (see p. 51 above). With reference to the later stages of his career, however, The Times History of the War states that 'he had not shown an aptitude for guerilla war and, like many other senior men, he had lost in energy under the strain and tedium of a long campaign'. The term 'rundling' seems to have been Jones's own coinage for 'muddling through'. The Cornelis River is situated between the towns of Vrede and Harrismith.

Pleasant Gift, 31st July 1901. I rode into Standerton on the 20th; the place is even more one-horse than ever. There was very little authentic news, but many rumours. Some said that Rundle had been Stellenbosched, others that he was to succeed

Kitchener. I heard that our division and Elliot's captured over 100 000 sheep, they are easier game than the Boers.

We marched back to De Lange's Drift on the 21st. It is a very evil spot now-a-days with the old camping grounds and dead beasts. We make matters still worse by our policy of burning the veldt wherever we go. No doubt there is a good deal to be said in favour of destroying the grass to annoy the Boer, but when it is done at regular halting places like the Drift we suffer far more than he does. I have never been on any trek in which the oxen had so bad a time as on this one. The grass is burnt, the cattle are most of them very young and weak, and the drivers are new hands and quite incompetent. The powers that be have quite made up their great minds that the trek ox is better without food; the regimental trek ox, that is the Staff animal, is differently treated. I have known our transport officer forbidden to take forage which was burnt a few minutes later.

The next three days were uneventful: we marched on the 22nd by Gruisplaatz to Tradouw, on the 23rd to Malta, and on the 24th to Botha's Berg, where I found myself once more on outpost on top of the mountain. There were a good many Boers about, and one day they managed to kill two Yeomen.

The 25th was a long day. We started at ten, the Regiment finding the rearguard. When it was past four we came on the convoy laagered up, and after three contra-dictory orders were told to be ready to march on at six. While we were snatching a hasty meal, the cow gun was firing at a range of 6000 yards into a little glen that we could just see the mouth of. I heard afterwards that it was the appearance of some fifty Boers in that direction which brought the column to a standstill. They had a number of Cape carts with them, so of course by all the laws of the game we had to give them a good start.

It was quite dark by the time the rear guard got off. The men, curiously enough, were in the highest spirits, but inclined to be sarcastic when they discussed the tactics of our leaders. Anyone who spoke at all loudly was cautioned not to wake the Boers. When you remember that three hundred Kaffirs were yelling like fiends in the endeavour to make their exhausted oxen move, the humour of the situation is apparent.

We entered the glen and camped on a slope like the roof of a house near a farm called Driehoek between ten and eleven, having marched well over twenty miles. The result? Goodness knows, but it was a magificent specimen of 'rundling'.

Next morning we found that the cow gun by four rounds (£150) had bagged a little foal. The poor beast was considerably scattered and a good many of the fragments were a bright canary yellow.

On the 26th we marched to the Cornelia or one its tributaries, I am not sure which. Most of the farms along the road were burnt and the kraals cleared out. We wound up the day by climbing down a kind of precipice to the river, appar-ently because the guide said the place was almost impassable. Very little grief was displayed when one of the great man's Mess wagons stood on its head half way down. I stayed on the top of the hill on outpost, a cold place, but I got at my wagon before anyone else. Two of our companies on the hills across the river never got their blankets at all.

This night we could see the fires of the 17th Brigade, which had parted from us on the 25th, on the Witte Kopjes six or seven miles away.

On the 27th we started at noon and marched west along the valley to our old camping ground about eight miles away. The 17th Brigade marched through part of our rear guard quite promiscuous like. I met a man on our hill and we swopped lies for some time before we discovered that we belonged to different brigades. The regimental officer is never told anything, and it is pure luck if he never fires on his friends.

On the 28th we made a short march to Verkyker's Kop. As usual, I was up the mountain. Rundling worse than ever, seven companies on outpost out of a total of thirteen.

There is a fine farm under the hill belonging to an Odendaal, a wealthy old man nicknamed 'Bantjes' (spelling and meaning uncertain); he was fined £400 for refusing to go on commando, and is one of the few men in the district who have kept their oath of neutrality. As we approached the farm, the Colonel, who commanded the advance guard, saw about forty Boers with led horses slipping away from it. The Yeomen were hunting chickens or something of the kind, and the Boers were gone before our leading company came up. The Odendaals were removed next day and the farm burnt, but the old man is to be compensated.

We marched towards three points of the compass in turn on the 29th, but eventually fetched up at Maaritz Drift on the Molen River, not very far from our starting point. A column of Guards was sent off to a farm called Pleasant Gift, and their outposts fought a great battle with ours on the morning of the 30th. In the afternoon we marched on four miles and joined them. I was on a kopje again that night.

To-day (31st) the column went two miles, and I went round to the other side of my kopje. There is a farm just below my camp which was burnt this morning, and my men have had a great day treasure hunting about it. Among the rocks on the hills they found all sorts of things – clothes and bedding, an autoharp (there is a concert going on at present), a fine marble clock, and a good pair of gem[s]bok's horns. I have the last. Near the farm some of them dug up a lot of plated things. They are quite convinced that if they could stay here a few days they would all make their fortunes.

1st August 1901. To Harrismith.

However, for all the boredom, routine, hardship and danger, there were consolations as well, quite apart from the odd pair of gemsbok horns, especially if one was an officer. At Ficksburg in the eastern Free State, for example, R.B. Pott spent considerable time and energy organising an officers' club.

Wednesday, 13th February 1901. A day off. Went to the Club and spent the whole

54. *'Self in office, Beaufort West.' The snapshot comes from the albums of E.S. Barrett, who was stationed in Beaufort West for the greater part of the war, and presumably shows Barrett himself; nothing further is known about him. Note especially the flowered wallpaper, the small Union Jack surmounting the map of the district, and the photograph of the Duke and Duchess of Cornwall and York (later King George V and Queen Mary), who visited the Cape in August 1901.* (INIL 2807)

day there until 4 o'clock, when I went to see the Worcester Mounted Infantry pass their drill before the Colonel. They passed 'with honours'. The G.O.C. in orders congratulated the Column on their work of the previous two days.

Engaged two Basuto boys at 30s. a month as Club waiters. Dined with the Colonel in the evening and played bridge.

Thursday, 14th February 1901. Again spent the day at the Club, to which arrived the G.O.C. to see how we were getting on. We have now nearly finished furnishing, but find we are short of the following: chairs, lamps, whisky, tea cups and long glasses.

In the evening went to a concert; on returning had 15 officers in my tent drinking whisky and soda and eating cake. This ended in a bear fight between Palmer and myself.

Friday, 15th February 1901. Yet another day at the Club, ably assisted by Howse, Elwes and Hardwick. Raised 7 chairs, 7 bottles of whisky and 3 lamps, but long glasses and tea cups unprocurable. Club opens to-morrow, Stafford band plays, and G.O.C. and Staff get free teas. What will be my fate for having failed to procure tea cups and long glasses? Short glasses will have to do, I think.

Played polo for an hour and a half on absolutely rotten ponies, Willow Grange having an awful back and Whisper being rather bad also.

Saturday, 16th February 1901. Spent the whole morning at the new Officers' Club, Ficksburg, giving finishing touches. Club opened in the afternoon, great function, band of the South Staffords played outside. General Officer Commanding and Staff came to tea. Some 30 or 40 members attended. The only mistake was that the milk for tea and the General Officer Commanding ran a dead heat, and I was horribly afraid at one time that the General Officer Commanding would have milkless tea. However, all went well, and everyone including the G.O.C. was very complimentary.

In the evening Major E.M. Perceval, Captains Hope and Elwes and Lt. Hardwick[1] dined with the West Kent Squadron officers. Elwes and I afterwards adjourned to the Club and played bridge with Colonel Firman and Ritchie, A.D.C.

An account of operations somewhat less exciting than those in which Jardine and Jones were involved was given by the 19-year-old Leslie Fortescue of the Imperial Yeomanry who was serving under Col. Hickie in the western Transvaal. Although De la Rey and his guerrilla forces were active here, only three columns were operating against them, under Methuen, Hickie and Kekewich respectively, while the greater part of the British military apparatus was concentrated on Botha and De Wet, and The Times History of the War *observes with regard to this period that 'for a long time past hostilities had languished in the western Transvaal'.*

The letter from young Fortescue to his brother quoted here is written on paper with printed columns headed 'No./Naam/Adres/Commando', annotated by him, 'I took this paper from the Boers we captured – rather interesting, is it not? L.F.' Little is known of him apart from the information in the small collection of letters for the period 1901-1902 of which this item forms part, but they are accompanied, evocatively if enigmatically, by a commercial pamphlet entitled 'How to become strong' and a lengthy manuscript note by an unknown writer beginning, 'One of the most remarkable events that happened at the School was when Leslie was Captain of the Junior Football Team, and with an acknowledged much weaker team won the Shield.'

Transvaal, 11.ix.01
6th Squad. Imp. Yeo., F. F., S. Africa
(Col. Hickie's Column)

My dear S., – Unfortunately for me I have been so messed about that I have not received a letter from you or Albert for some considerable time. I joined this

1. Note in the original: 'This officer was my greatest friend. He was killed at Tweefontein on Christmas Day 1901, being riddled by bullets while gallantly serving his pom-pom against overwhelming odds.'

55. 'Native orderlies, B.W.', another snapshot from the Barrett Albums, taken at Beaufort West. Many black men were involved in the war, both directly and indirectly, though little publicity was given to the fact at the time. (INIL 2826)

Column with the 6th Squadron owing to one of their sergeants being in hospital, so I came in charge of one of their troops very much against my wish, as the responsibilities of a sergeant are great. He has since rejoined, and I am expecting orders daily to rejoin the 12th Regiment.

I received a letter from the Pater dated 10th October, for which kindly thank him. He asked me the somewhat difficult question of what is my position in the Yeomanry. I take it that I am still on the Staff of the 12th, but owing to circumstances over which I had no control I have been placed on other duties, in fact by the time I have finished I shall have had a very varied experience of active service. My proper position is with the Staff of the 12th Regiment, and by all accounts I have no right to be [here?] at all.

The Pater also seems anxious that I should leave the Yeomanry with a commission. If I was willing to waste £60 or so, I would apply for one, and the chances are that I should be successful, as I have already been provisionally approved for same by Col. de Rougemont, which would go a long way with Lord Chesham. I cannot keep up a commission as it should be kept up on 8s. per day. I have seen others try to do [so], but they have failed miserably. It is most essential that I should look at

56. *A nurse and (presumably) two medical orderlies, another snapshot taken in the Imperial Yeomanry Hospital at Elandsfontein.* (INIL 2857)

these matters from a financial point of view, is it not?

To return to business. I have now had three weeks' experience of Col. Hickie, and I must say I have found him a very warm customer. He combines the two essential qualities in warfare, caution and dash. We are only a small column of 500 or 600 strong, and we are operating in a country swarming with Boers; where they all come from is a mystery to me. Some nights he will have as many as 400[?][2] men on outpost and picket; this makes it terribly hard work for the men.

Last night we obtained news that De la Ray was going to attack us with 700 men. We saddled up about half past eleven at night, and took up a position in [*sic*] a koppie about 2 miles from camp and there awaited the expected attack, but fortunately for the Boers they, I suppose, decided to postpone it, as after a tedious and cold vigil of six hours we returned to the camp without even firing a shot. I venture to say that if we had been attacked the Boers would have got one of the warmest receptions they have had for some considerable time. It is weird and trying work, moving about in a hostile country at night. No one is allowed to speak or smoke to break the stillness of the night.

Our squadron had a dust-up with the Boers a few days ago. We drove them from

2. The paper has been damaged here and the first digit is not clearly legible.

a strong position on a bush-covered koppie. Whether they suffered much we do not know. We had no casualties on our own side, although two or three close things.

On another occasion half a troop under my command had orders to search a koppie supposed to be occupied by Boers. We rode up the koppie, which was covered with large stones. I had just given the order to dismount and proceed to the top of the koppie on foot when a couple of Boers appeared within 10 yards of us, but before they could do any damage they were covered by our rifles. We took them prisoners and searched the ground for rifles and ammunition. We had evidently caught them asleep or we should not have got so far up the koppie – they were so well hid that it was impossible to see them.

The weather is most trying; it has rained or hailed near every day we have been on trek, for you have doubtless read of hail stones as big as turkey eggs. We had a storm last Monday when I can say without the slightest exaggeration that many of the hail stones were as large and some larger than turkey eggs, and by jove, if one of them happens to catch you on the head, you know it, I can tell you. It is no joke riding through hail storms, which we have had to do on several occasions lately. I must say that we do see life in this country, what say you, old boy? It is a grand feeling galloping for all you are worth to the foot of a koppie, but it is rather past a joke when you have to climb up a hundred feet or so with possibly some Boer lead to help you on the way.

They tell me that the Yeomanry mobilise for home in January. I rather doubt it. I have got rather chary of believing these rumours.

I was interested in the Pater's account of Clara's wedding. I hope they will be happy.

We march in a few minutes, so must close.

Sincerely, hoping you are all well at home, and that I shall have the pleasure of hearing from you shortly. With love and best wishes, believe me, your affectionate brother, Leslie.

The boredom, constant danger and erratic, infrequent moments of excitement described by young Fortescue are probably typical of what the average British soldier experienced during the period of guerrilla warfare. A broadly similar picture is given by M.W. Tyler, who by the late winter of 1901 was stationed at Rooikraal in the Middelburg Tvl. district. Being attached to the military hospital services, he was, of course, behind the lines, insofar as this concept can be applied to guerrilla warfare, and the boredom was consequently greater, especially after the excitement he had experienced in Ladysmith during the siege.

The 'Burgher Scouts' mentioned by Tyler were surrendered Boers in the employ of the British military authorities. 'General Kitchener' was of course not the Commander-in-Chief, but Maj. Genl. Walter Kitchener, to whose column Tyler was at this time attached: on 29 July Kitchener surprised the commando of Genl. C.H. Muller in the Blood River valley, Natal, and took 32 prisoners (even modest achievements had become important at this stage of the war).

The extract given below also provides some more incidental information on relations between white and black during the war.

11.8.01. Convoy left at 7 a.m., and I moved about and got the lines cleaned up. One Kaffir being disposed to dispute authority was ordered six strokes on his bare bottom.

12.8.01. Got up early and rode over to Devon Regt. Heard that Col. Parke had found two Maxims.

Burgher Scouts brought in seven prisoners. Convoy from flying column came in with news that our General was pursuing Muller's commando and had left all supplies at Crocodile drift under one officer and 60 men 1st Devons. Two companies are therefore to march out to reinforce this party to hold the drift at all cost.

13.8.01. Saw convoy march off at 7 a.m. Col. Campbell inspected our camp today at 10 a.m.

We amused ourselves by moving all the hospital tents forward about 20 yards.

14.8.01. Up at 7.a.m. Suffering from severe cold. Felt very heavy and drowsy. Absolutely no news and nothing to do, time hangs heavy.

15.8.01. Usual day of idleness. Went over to Mitchell's place, and returned and read *Times* of July 5th. Hearing some good news had come in, sent to B.O. for it. There were five sheets. In one of which was a statement that the Troop in South Africa sent from India would be replaced at an early date.

16.8.01. A perfect day's misery. No one in our camp to speak to; so I went over to Mitchell's place.

On being asked to play cards last evening, I declined. One of our Blk. A.S.'s [sic] asked if I was afraid of losing. I replied 'No', and expressed my view that [he] had never had so much money before in his life. At which he took offence, so we don't speak as we pass bye.

Rooi Kraal. 17.8.01. Went over to Devon Regiment and played a game of whist, Essex against the world, Essex being represented by myself from Chelmsford and Sergeant Green, Devon Regiment, from Manningtree. The world was defended by Sergt Bird and Sergt Coombes, Devons, the latter winning by one rubber.

Convoy from Flying Column came in. No news.

18.8.01. Sent out convoy to Column which returned, not being required. General expected back tomorrow or 20th inst.

19.8.01. News received from Genl. Kitchener. 19th Hussars had an engagement with Muller's commando and were nearly surrounded, but 18th Hussars came up and saved the situation. We have 10 casualties, 5 killed and 5 wounded, and lost the carriage of Colt gun and 35 horses. Boers driven off with heavy losses(?).

20.8.01. General with column returned. Convoy to Diep Kloof.

21.8.01. Marched to Diep Kloof.

22.8.01. West Australians' sports. I played a game of tip and run cricket today. Sing-song at night.

57. British war graves in an unidentified cemetery: a dry-stone wall, five crosses, some wreaths and an empty jam tin, with a boy in paramilitary dress planting his foot on a heap of earth in a proprietary way, and the shadow of the photographer and his camera immortalised in the left foreground. (Hess Album)

Bleaker still was the lot of James Bell from Glasgow, who by the end of 1901 had progressed from Modder River to guard duty at one of the blockhouses which had sprung up throughout South Africa during the course of the year. They were part of Kitchener's grand plan to make it impossible for Boer commandoes to move freely about the country, and by the conclusion of the war they numbered no fewer than 8000. The location of No. 63 blockhouse has not been traced.

The Exhibition referred to was held in Glasgow. The excitements of Bell's life in South Africa were of a much lesser order.

63 Blockhouse, 15 Decr. 1901

Dear Mother, – I got your welcome letters alright, also the present, but the pipe and socks that Mary speaks of have not yet come to hand, but may do so later on.

The Exhibition seems to have been a great success and brought a great many people about the town, and ought to have done a great deal of good to the trade of the town.

Things are very quiet here just now, we have not heard of any Boers being in the vicinity for the last few months, but there is no saying when they may turn up.

God knows when it's going to end, sometime in the far future, judging by the rate of progress just now.

I am keeping in good health and am feeling better than I ever did since I came to the country, that is on account of the regular living we have here. We have 1/4 lb fresh beef, 1/4 lb bread, 1/2 lb vegetables (potatoes and onions mixed), 1/3 oz. tea, 1 oz. coffee, 3 ozs. sugar and 1/4 lb jam per man per day, and 1/2 gill rum twice a week.

We have absolutely nothing to do except two hours sentry go in the night, so you may imagine the life we are living.

The authorities supplied us with all kinds of seeds, and we are trying to grow vegetables and flowers, but I am afraid we won't have enough of spare water to make a success.

This is all the news this time, so I wish you all at home a merry Christmas and a happy New Year. Your affectionate son, James.

It may be remembered that in the winter of 1900, Ford S. Barclay, writing from the newly occupied Johannesburg, had speculated on 'the early finish of the war': 'I shouldn't be much surprised if we didn't get it over by Xmas' (p. 59 above). By Christmas 1901, Bell was remarking despondently, 'God knows when it's going to end, sometime in the far future.' In the event, both men were inaccurate in their predictions, but the British view of the conflict had obviously changed dramatically during the course of eighteen months.

58. (opposite). 'The invasion of the Colony: the Malmesbury contingent of the W.P.M.R. under Lieut. Lawrence, en route from Van Rhynsdorp to their homes. The majority of these men are loyal Dutch colonists' (detail). The Western Province Mounted Riflemen was one of the units involved in local defence after the second invasion of the Cape Colony by Boer forces in December 1900. (Cape Times Weekly, 29.5.1901)

THE WAR
PROTRACTED
(1900-1902)

*A*s the British army moved into the Republics, the situation in the Cape Colony became increasingly tense and the ambivalent loyalties of the white population grew steadily more apparent. Emotions were aroused especially by the trials of the Cape rebels who had joined the Boer forces during the early months of the war, while a strong movement in favour of the annexation of the Republics developed among the pro-British party.

At the beginning of May 1900, when Bloemfontein had been occupied and Roberts' march northward just resumed, the Magistrate of Graaff-Reinet reported as follows by telegraph to the authorities in Cape Town regarding the local situation. Walter Rubidge, who is mentioned with some asperity, was a prominent local farmer whose life was later described as 'one of ceaseless activity and hard work in his own interests and in those of the farming community around him'; he had been a candidate in the elections of 1895 and had been defeated by the Afrikaner Bond. The explosion in Johannesburg referred to had actually occurred at Begbie's Foundry on 24 April, while a local appeal had been made at the Cape on behalf of those affected by a disastrous fire in Canada.

Secretary to the Law Department, Cape Town. May 1st, 1900. 159. Confidential. District is quiet. There is not even any talk in the town, chiefly because there is no special news from the front and because Mr Walter Rubidge's very aggressive loyalty is at present quiescent, his energies being directed to social duties connected with the presence of the Regiment of Sherwood Foresters here. The news of the explosion of the arsenal at Johannesburg and the fire at Ottawa in Canada were great shocks, but men's minds centre upon the war.

Graaff-Reinet was, however, in the heart of an Afrikaans-speaking district of dubious allegiance, and on 31 May a Volkskongres or 'People's Congress' was held there at which more than a thousand people met to protest against the war. Further public meetings and demonstrations were to be held throughout the Cape Colony by supporters of both the British and Boer sides, but for the remainder of the year the precarious neutrality was maintained, and for most people life went on much as usual.

Three contemporary letters by unknown individuals writing about their trivial personal concerns are quoted here, even though none of them even mentions the war. In the first place these letters indicate how everyday life was continuing in the Cape Colony during the late winter and spring of 1900, while the British were attempting to estab-

59. 'The People's Congress at Graaff-Reinet (The pro-Boer organ says there were 2,500 people present. We leave the public to judge).' The Congress, called to protest against the war, took place on 31 May 1900; the 'pro-Boer organ' was the Cape Town newspaper Ons Land. (Cape Argus Weekly, 13.6.1900)

lish control over the Republics, H.R. Langmore and his companions were bayonetting pigs and removing livestock from farms in the western Transvaal and J.H. Kuhlmann in Pretoria was tentatively planning his future. Quite apart from this, however, these random items give an indication of the wide range of materials in the manuscript collections of the South African Library which deal with 'ordinary' people and everyday events and provide information on the fabric of South Africa's past.

The first of these letters was written from Krakeel River in the lower Langkloof in the vicinity of George, where the writer, Thys van Huysteen, had obviously set up as a general dealer. It has been preserved among the papers of Charles Searle, to whom it was sent by the addressee, J.C. Saayman of Uniondale, at the Houses of Parliament in Cape Town, from which one infers that Searle had taken an interest in Van Huysteen or was somehow involved in his affairs. Once again attention must be drawn to the phenomenon of Dutch-speaking people preferring to write to one another in stilted English.

Krakeel River, 21.9.1900

Dear Oom Jaap, – Yours safely to hand. The invoice I went through a little and found a small error thus far, you have 4 pipes at 2s. and 2 at 1/6, it is really 2 at 2s. and 4 at 1/6. I will look it over again to see whether it is correct.

Groceries I am glad to say is going very slow. I don't think I sold one bag of coffee yet. Flour I have never touched yet. It is mostly soft goods the people are buying. I have nearly £35 in hand. The people here don't bother much about credit. I have sold for about £11 or £12 on credit. That is nearly £50 I have sold in a week's time.

They don't either bother about the prices. It seems to me Cooper had a good time of it before I came here. Whenever one of them buy[s] things say for about 7/6 or 8/6, I remind them about the discount I give if they buy for 10s. or £1. Believe me they do feel pleased to get discount.

You must forward goods I ordered without delay, for I am out in many lines, as for instance vinegar, saucepans, cups and saucers, basins, etc., etc. I am enclosing another small order of goods I forgot the other day.

A waggon left here for Willowmore last night, he will bring goods if it be ready when he returns. Coffee and sugar you can only send a few bags of each. People like best coffee most, but I think it advisable to keep both qualities. With kindest regards, yours sincerely, M. van Huysteen.

Cango tobacco is selling off well. Don't forget to send sole leather.

A similar letter, in that it relates to local and commercial affairs on the platteland, was written at about the same time by Henry Theron of Fraserburg. It was addressed to Charles Earp, who for twelve years had been a shopkeeper in that isolated village, moving to Cape Town with his family in the 1890s, where he was connected with the family firm Maxwell & Earp, general merchants and importers.

Theron's English was fluent but faulty; his letter is reproduced unaltered. Fraserburg Road (now Leeu-Gamka) was the nearest railway station, 130 kilometres away. It will be noted that the war does not yet seem to have impinged on Fraserburg in any way, although Theron may have refrained deliberately from commenting on it: Earp's sentiments were pro-British, and he was to be among those attending the two-day conference of the South African Vigilance Committee held in Cape Town later that month.

Fraserburg, Aug. 9th, 1900

My dear Mr Earp, – Yours of the 5th inst. duly to hand, for which I must thank you. It was delightfull to hear from you again, it always reminds me of the past.

Re what I mentioned to you in my last letter, I have not heard from my brother yet, therefore I have not decided on any thing yet. As I have mentioned, Mrs van Rensburg is wishing to give me money, but she cannot, it is not here. Therefore I want to ask you to do me the favour of giving me a letter of recommendation to prove what I can do. I shall be very much oblige if you can let me have same at your earliest convenience, as I might require same. Should you know of any place that I am fit for, I shall be glad if you will let me know.

I want to ask Conradie for one as well. I wonder whether he will give me one. I don't think he will refuse me.

They are having a dance in the Court Room this evening. I don't think they will have many ladies.

The passenger wagon leaves here Tuesday morning and leaves Fraserburg Road Thursday afternoon, single fair 30s., return ticket 40s. The post cart came down to the same prices. I heard the passenger wagon is coming to an end, they find it does not pay.

Wm Olivier of Rooihuevel are have a sale of all his goods. I wonder why. Conradie left last Tuesday for Cape Town.

Hopeing to hear soon from you. Kindest regards to Mrs Earp and the children. Yours faithfully, Henry Theron.

Theron does not seem to have succeeded in his attempt to get away from Fraserburg, for on the voters' roll of 1903 he is listed as clerk to the local shopkeeper P.J. Viviers.

A boy's eye view of Cape Town at the turn of the century is given in a letter by Charles Earp's son Errol, twelve years of age, to his mother, Emma Earp, who was away from home; Kathleen, Olive and Donald were his sisters and brother. Emma Earp was a younger sister of Katie Stuart (see p. 60 above), and the Earp children were therefore members of the Schreiner family complex, Olive Earp having been named after her great-aunt. Sabiena, whose personal affairs are treated in such a cavalier fashion, was presumably the maid.

'Fair View', Rondebosch, 17 October 1900

Dear Mother, – I hope you were not displeased when you received no letter from me.

Kathleen is now at this present moment yelling 'It is, it is', besides throwing things of all sorts at my head, simply because I said drawing was not painting.

Do you know I am also going on a trip to recruit my health with your leave. Father thinks we will leave on the 5th of November for Sir Lowry's pass and arrive at Caledon on the same evening. Stay there for a day or two, then to Bedarsdorp [*sic*], Swellendam, Robertson, Worcester and home, a nice little trip, what do you think?

I have been repairing one of my men-of-war to-day. She has three leaks which I have mended with putty. I asked Father to find out for me the price of twelve men belonging to the 1st Life Guard band. What do you think, they cost 9/6 for the lot. Isn't it awful? Why! I could get 48 Infantry soldiers or 30 Cavalry for the same amount.

We are looking forward to your coming home with great delight. My whooping cough is over I might almost say. Our [*sic*] is Olive, well, I hope. Tell her I am

60. Olive, Errol and Kathleen Earp, a studio photograph taken in about 1900. (INIL 13686)

expecting a letter from her. I have got a book for my cigarette coupons.

I have got to go to the Library to-day, so I must leave off. Bye-the-bye, Sabiena sends her love and says she's better, also her Father died of influenza. Kathleen, Donald and myself send love. Errol.

Shortly before this letter was written, a women's protest meeting against the war had been held at Somerset East, to which Olive Schreiner had sent a rousing message, and there was still considerable Boer activity in the southern Free State. While young Errol was happily occupied with his toy soldiers and men-of-war, however, the war was developing into something more than a matter of discussion and debate for the people of the Cape Colony.

After the fall of the Republican capitals it soon became clear to the Boer commandoes remaining in the field that they would not be able to hold out for long against the mass onslaught of the British. In order to provide some diversion and relief, Free State forces on 16 December 1900 therefore once again invaded the Cape Colony, but this time in a more forceful and purposeful way than at the beginning of the war. Before long almost the entire colony had become directly involved in the guerrilla war: martial law was proclaimed in all districts except the seaports and the 'native territories' of the eastern Cape, the towns and villages were turned into armed fortresses, and Boer commandoes, their numbers strengthened by Cape rebels, roamed at will over the countryside, penetrating as far south as Darling.

During this extremely uncertain time, Thomas Searle, a member of the prominent Searle family of Great Brak River and brother of the Member of Parliament Charles Searle, was in constant contact with Captain J.W. Robinson, the British Intelligence Officer at Swellendam, and the Commandants at Mossel Bay and George. His voluminous correspondence with them seems to have been intended to provide proof of his loyalty, and he described himself in a letter as 'a private individual working voluntarily and gratuitously to find out information that might be of value to you in checkmating the enemy' (19.9.1901). On being informed rather testily by Robinson that 'What I want from you is information more political than military' and having been accused of 'partiality', he defended himself and his loyalty in an eloquent letter of three and a half typed folio pages, from which the following is taken. It gives a fair enough picture of the position in which the loyalist inhabitants of the Cape Colony found themselves during the period of the Boer invasion.

Great Brak River, Sept. 24, 1901

(. . .) I should like to say that I am not actuated in anything I do by trade interests. These certainly lie all in the direction of 'heart-whole devotion to the cause of peace', as we are losing heavily every day this unrest keeps up, and if for no other reason you should believe that I am sincere in my wishes for peace. But I have always tried to do what is *right*, irrespective of trade interests, and trust I have at all events to some extent succeeded.

As for my loyalty, I do not know what more I can do to show it. It was born in me and has been part of my religion all my life. I have defended even questionable acts through the war through thick and thin. My only son old enough, a lad of barely 15 years, has lived in the George trenches for three weeks and has been in the Town Guard almost since its formation. Our manager at George has been in charge of one of the forts, our head man at Mossel Bay has also been in military service for more than a month, we supplied at great inconvenience nine cyclists to Mossel Bay when they were badly wanting them, and they were away a month, until their services were no longer required. I myself have been for the last three weeks or more simply working day and night almost to scout and get information for the Military. I have preached loyalty, denounced disloyalty and done all that mortal man can do to show my love for King and Country. Well, if I am suspected, God pity others!

Excuse my writing strongly, but I can assure you even suspicion of not being thoroughly loyal wounds me to the quick.

(. . .)

The next two items, likewise from the correspondence of Thomas Searle, plunge straight into the practical implications of the guerrilla war, and deal with the spring of 1901, when a Boer commando pursued by the British crossed the Outeniqua mountains and the village of Great Brak River was briefly threatened.

The following report of suspicious activities in this area was sent to Searle by a local inhabitant during this period. The surname Terblans or Terblanche was at that time very common in the area, and at least two men with the corresponding initials occur on the voters' rolls: a farmer in the Outeniqua Division and a general dealer in the Division of Brak River. In the latter there was also a coloured labourer named Willem Willemse living at Klipheuvel, who may well be the man referred to by Terblans, but the name transcribed tentatively as 'Frumershum' is not very legible in the original.

The writer was obviously not an educated man and his phonetic Dutch gives the impression that he may have been coloured, but probably he was merely reproducing dialectical forms common among Afrikaans-speakers in the area. [Translation on pp. 159-160.]

Mr Tom Searle, G.B.R. – Heer heef een report gekom van Frumershum[?] dat Wellem Wellems en nog meer van de ander menchen, dat zulle daar eits gezein heef tegen de Berg omtrent 2 meel van de Waterwerk, dat heef hem gescheen of het leevindege goed is, en so als dit van feer af lijk, kan dit omtrent 30 man wees. Ik was niet en kans om te gaan kyk, want het was donker, maar ik heef zulle georder om van nag wag te hoe, en als zulle eets gewaar, om dat dadelyk te kom report. U kan no[u] verder denk wat goed is om verder te doen. C.J. Terblans, H.C.

Another, similar letter is anonymous and the address has been carefully effaced, although the reference 'hier op Kleynvaley' in the text has been overlooked. The names mentioned appear to refer to the commando of J.L.Theron, which was stated by the British Intelligence Service towards the end of the war to consist of 'Mostly Transvaalers, big men, few youngsters, and about 30 unarmed coloured boys. (. . .) About one-third of the commando are Colonial Rebels, all unarmed.' Theron himself was described by the same source as 'Wanted for the murder of two natives, Swellendam District, 16th September, 1901', which refers to the period under discussion here, and he was stated to have the reputation of being 'cruel', all of which helps to explain the secrecy and fear surrounding these informal reports to the authorities. [Translation on p. 160.]

61. Thomas Searle of Great Brak River, a studio portrait with a flower in his buttonhole, taken by Fripp in Cape Town. (Searle Albums)

[*place deleted*], 20.9.1901

To Tos. Searle, Esq., Brakrivier. – Waarde heer, terwyl u aan my gezegt heeft dat ons Comedant gaarne eets weld weet wat die Boeren hier op Kleynvaley gesproken heeft aangaande die oorlog, ik ben zeker die mees wat hier gesproken es, was tegen my, want Cornelis was een presenier, zulle heeft hem gezegt om niet van zijn huis wegt te gaan, zoo was ik beeter enstand om eets te hoor.

Wat ik u zegt, kund U neem voor die geheele waarheid, ik zal die menschen geen onwaarheid ten laste legt, maar we moet aan ons Comedand vraag om niet met mijn naam openlijk te komen, daar die menschen gezegt heeft als wij hun raport, zal zulle ons plaatse afbrand, en wy kund nog ander gefolge te wagte wees.

Aan gaande ons gesprek, nu [sic] dat ik mijn kinders gewaarschouw heeft dat wij die menschen niets magt geeft, heeft ik onder gegaan na die oude weduwee haar huis om die menschen die selfte te zegt. Toen ik daar uitkwam, was het zoo donker, toen ontmoet ik een klompie van hun op die werf. Toen zegt ik aan hun zulle heeft ons en een slegte polittie [sic] geplaats om en ons Colonie te kom oorlog maak, zulle kon tog zeker geen hoop heb om die over wenneng te kryg moet die zwake magt. Toen zegt een van hun zulle heeft nu meer mannen als toen die oorlog begind heeft. Toen vraag een van hun door welke brel ik lees, of ik dan niet kan en zien dat zulle oorlog voer uit Engeland zijn zak.

Verder kon ik niet te horen kome of zulle Comandes van elkander weet, maar een heeft gezegt zulle weet alles wat en England aan gaan. Die verder gesprek was van geen belange.

Verder zoo ver ik van die namen weet, es als volg: Comedant Theron, Lefttennand De Vos, Joubert, Lombaard, Boshoff, 2 Nels, Obryns of soo omtrend, Hellibrand, Louwrens.

No less energetic than Thomas Searle in doing his bit during this time was Charles D. Hopkins of Paarl. Hopkins was an Afrikaans-speaking South African by birth, although his father had been an English immigrant, and he had been working in Johannesburg before the war as share broker and commission agent. The C.D. Hopkins Collection at the South African Library consists largely of documents dealing with this period in his life, but also includes personal reminiscences of the Transvaal under the title 'The Anglo-Boer War: Its Origin and its Consequences', which appear to have been compiled by him as well.

During the period of the Boer invasion of the Cape Colony, Hopkins wrote to the military commandant at Paarl requesting authorisation 'to demand from anyone a certain pamphlet circulated in Paarl this morning, containing a dream of some young girl', a manuscript copy of which was obtained, together with an English translation. Young Anna Kloppers, the girl concerned, seems to have been somewhat worked up as a result of war rumours and local pro-Boer gossip, on which her imagination elaborated, using what was probably the only imagery available in her restricted world, that of the Bible. The result is a confused medley of scriptural reminiscences, to which two Vierkleurs have been arbitrarily added, and it is hard to believe that anyone could have taken it seriously.

While Hopkins may have been over-zealous or over-officious, it is well to remember that this episode occurred in October 1901: Gideon Scheepers had recently been captured in the Prince Albert district and Hans Lotter and over fifty of his men sentenced to death or life imprisonment at Cradock; Hendrik Lategan was active in the Richmond area and J.C. Smuts was rumoured to be in the vicinity of Somerset West. Although the invaders never came near Paarl, it was a period of very real danger, tension and insecurity, as this incident helps recall.

The dream appears to have been written out by an adult, in not very good Dutch, from the dictation of Anna Kloppers herself. [Translation on p. 161.]

Een droom

Ik, Anna Kloppers, 12 jaar out, droomde ter midder nacht dat ik bij onze meddel deur en kwam en ik zag een zeer groot man en die voordeur staan, een losse mantel om zijne schouders hangende tot op zijne vouten. Op zijn hoofd had hij een kroon schittrend van diamanten, en zijne handen droig hij een brandende pot en kwam rook uit, wit zoo wit als snouw, die reg op Hemel waarst ging. Aan bijde zijden der pot was een vier kleur vlag.

Ik werd toen bevreesd. Hij merkte het en zijde, Zijt niet bevrees. Toen riep ik mijne moeder. Zij vroeg hem wie hij was. Hij zeide, Ik ben Michael. Zij vroeg hem waar heen hij reisde. Hij zeide, Ik kom van Ladijsmith en ben op reis naar de O.V.S. Hij zeide verder, Ziet gij deze pot, het is reuk werk op het altaar dat ik dag en nacht brandend houd, dei offer brengen de overwinneng voor die genen die zoo veel voor Christus' naam geleden hebben. De rook was prachtig wit als sneeuw en het had een heerlijke reuk. De rook dwaalde niet ront, maar steeg reg op Hemelwaarts.

Hij zeide tot mijne moeder, Lees Psalm 110 van vers 5, daar zult gij zien dat dit kleine volk niet vernietig zal worden. Nog een teks uit de profetiën, De Heer is een sterke toevlucht, enz., Hij zal met pentelentiën [*sic*] komen en zij zullen weten dat ik de Heere ben.

Toen zeide mijne moeder, Kom toch een weinig rusten, doch hij zeide, De vogelen des Hemels hebben nesten, maar wij hebben niets waar het hoofd neer te leggen. Ik ben de Alfa en Omiga, er is een begin gemaakt aan deze oorlog, ik zal er ook een einde aan maaken, ik heb het gezwooren en zal het doen.

In Paarl as at Great Brak River the war remained mainly a matter of rumour, uncertainty and expectation, but for the greater part of the Cape Colony the year 1901 was a time of violence, looting, raids, skirmishes and armed attacks, in which white and black, civilians and military suffered equally. A graphic account of the violence which by this time had become routine is provided by Captain H.A.P. Soppitt of the Loyal North Lancashire Regiment in a letter to an unidentified Colonel Mackie about an encounter between a British patrol and a Boer commando in the Stormberg district of the north-eastern Cape.

Soppitt's somewhat fulsome letter was intended to inform the Colonel of the not particularly remarkable conduct of his son under attack. To a later reader it is of interest in that it conveys something of what it must have felt like to be out in the field at the time, and even more for the rather casual reference to the shooting of the 'two nigger boys' in British employ.

Stormburg, 28.11.01

Dear Col. Mackie, – I feel I must write to you and tell you what took place yesterday morning to your son's credit.

Col. Salmond left here on the 26th about 2.30 p.m. with a patrol of 26 of our Regiment in an easterly direction. Major Cowper was down here inspecting us and he went out in my place. Well, I heard no more till 2.30 p.m. yesterday afternoon, when one of our men got back saying that the M[ounted] I[nfantry] had been in action and had been defeated. I rode out in that direction at once, and found a sergeant on his way back who informed me that George was behind him. The particulars are these.

Salmond (Commandant here) went out about 20 miles east of here on the way to Jamestown, and took up a position for the night, expecting to find a small party of Boers in the early morning. Sentries had to be placed, and George took his turn with the men at sentry go. Well, about 4.30 a.m. four Boers crossed below them. They fired and wounded one (since dead). The wounded man got away, but was eventually captured and brought back by your son. Of a sudden the kopje above them opened out a hot fire on our fellows. Col. Salmond ordered George to go out and bring in three horses which were loose and belonged to us. This he did promptly under a hot fire. One man named Fisher, seeing him with three horses, rushed out to help him, and was soon shot in the spine and died very quickly. After this the firing became tremendous. We have since found out that the commando under Van der Merve numbered 100.

George stuck to his post like a man, refusing to surrender, and about 11.30 he and Major Cowper found two or three Boers about 15 yards off them shouting 'Hands up!' Of course they had to obey, being left by themselves. The Boers took everything from them, their field glasses, watches, money, water bottles, haversack[s], putties and everything, in fact nearly stripped them. George had one bullet cut his breeches at the knee, but was not grazed at all. Another bullet cut his boot and a splinter cut his boot also. Cowper was hit in the bandolier but not hurt. Then they had to walk back 23 miles altogether to get here, both almost done up, and today I have kept him in bed, and I think tomorrow he will be as fit as ever again.

This was not your son's first baptism of fire, but it was his first serious one, and Major Cowper and all tell me he behaved *splendidly*, he was as cool as a cucumber and gave his order of command perfectly. I felt I must write and tell you all about it, because I know what a modest chap he is, he would probably hardly mention it.

Our total casualties are one killed and four wounded, including Col. Salmond and Lt. Lyon of the 3rd East Surrey, [and] two nigger boys who were taken out to hold the horses &c. and were shot in cold blood, placed against a wall and murdered. Poor old George is naturally upset, but will soon be all right again, and no doubt he will write to you further particulars. I hope this may hasten his commission, though I do not want to part with him, as he is such a friend of mine and such a good soldier, but I am doing my best with the C.O. about him, and so is Major Cowper.

Believe me to remains yours truly, (sgd.) H.A.P. Soppitt, Comdg. Detacht 3rd Loyal North Lancs.

62. 'Shooting a native (from a photograph).' No further information is provided, although the illustration accompanies text which mentions the capture and shooting 'in cold blood' of a 'native policeman' by the commando of P.H. Kritzinger outside Willowmore on 18 January 1901. (From, H.W. Wilson: After Pretoria; vol.1 (1902))

The Boer forces were particularly active in the arid and sparsely populated Namaqualand district, where they were able to move about freely. The following account describes the visit of Manie Maritz and his commando to the Wesleyan mission settlement of Leliefontein in the Kamiesberg, and the unexpected resistance put up by the coloured inhabitants. The 25-year-old Maritz had newly been promoted to the rank of general by J.C. Smuts and commanded more than 500 men who were in virtual control of the Calvinia and Kenhardt districts.

Among the black population of the Cape Colony feelings against the Boers were particularly strong. Black men, not allowed to participate formally in the war, played an active role in the town guards formed to assist in local defence, and also acted as scouts, spies and informers: some 300 Leliefontein men are, for example, estimated to have been employed as scouts by the Namaqualand Intelligence Department, which exposed them to summary justice at the hands of the Boers when captured. Of the Cape rebels sentenced to death during this period, many were charged with murder as well as treason, for arbitrary executions of this type were often carried out.

The community at Leliefontein was at this time reasonably large and prosperous: the voters' roll for 1903 lists 31 male voters, all of whom are designated 'Hottentots' and described as owners of property, while almost all are listed as farmers. Among the

127

63. 'Promulgation of sentence on rebels, Cradock', a commercial photograph from the album of Lawrence Richardson, who also provided the caption. It was taken on 12 July 1901, and shows the public promulgation of sentence on the Cape rebel J.P. Coetzee, who was hanged at Cradock three days later. (INIL 10675)

names are those of several members of the Dirks family, including 'John Dirks', whose occupation is given as storekeeper, Barnabas Shaw Links and Barnabas Jacobus Links. The Revd Barnabas Shaw had been the founder of the mission, and the Khoi Jacob Links was one of his first converts and helpers. As the people are likely to have spoken a form of Afrikaans by this time, it is not clear what is meant by Barnabas Links speaking to his men 'in his own language'.

This account was obviously written by one of Maritz's followers, who was well educated and had a good command of English, but its author and provenance are both unknown. There is a clean copy among the papers of the Revd J.G. Locke of Leliefontein (see p. 134 below) headed 'Copy of some papers found at Concordia after its evacuation by the Boers on the 2nd May 1902', as well as a single-leaf printed edition with the same heading, in both of which the name 'Lilyfountain' has been altered to 'Leliesfontein'. As this printed version is not widely known, the text has been regarded as a manuscript for the purposes of inclusion in this collection.

General Maritz and seven other men left Korenlandskloof on the morning of the 24th of January [1902]. The General's intention was to go to Comdt Schoeman's laager, which was at Grootvlei at the time.

Before going further, I must acquaint the reader with the distances of the various places concerned in our little story. The distance between Korenlandskloof and Lilyfontain is 6 miles, between Lilyfountain and Grootvlei about 24. I must further mention that the General's commando, with which he had come from the district of Calvinia and which was under the direct command of Comdt Kampfer, was that day at Doornkraal, i.e. 18 miles from Lilyfountain. It is thus clear that the nearest help in case of danger was 18 miles off, and that in a mountainous and difficult country to travel.

As was said before, we left Korenlandskloof and reached Lilyfountain at about 9 o'clock that morning, where we descended from the stony hill to the west of the location into its precincts. We were met by a certain Jan Dirks. On seeing us, he approached, and in a very respectful manner took off his hat to say 'Goodmorning.' Then everybody looked so peaceful, women and children were seen going in and out their homesteads, men formed into little groups to talk to each other, and everything had the appearance of peace.

The General now began to talk to Jan Dirks. On his question whether the Missionary was at home, Dirks said 'No', but that for the time being he was his substitute. The General then told him who he was and that he meant to do them no harm, but that on the contrary he would severely punish any of his men who without provocation might do any of them the least bit of injustice.

He further told him that he had a proclamation which he, Jan Dirks, could read to the other natives of the station. He, however, slyly and treacherously invited the General to come to the Missionary's house to read the proclamation to all of them there in front of the parsonage. He assented to read the proclamation to all of them, but fortunately went to the side of the church, where in the shadow of its wall we stopped our horses and dismounted. I said 'fortunately', because their armed men all lay in the garden in front of the parsonage, where behind the stone walls they had their fort.

In the meantime Jan Dirks had gathered his men, who were now swarming round us, to listen to our proclamation. Among the encircling audience was recognized the face of Barnabas Linksch as one of the natives captured at Garies by Field Cornet Rudolph in September 1901, who as it was thought now had, according to his oath, come to live in peace at Lilyfountain and keep himself to his parole.

Before the proclamation was read, Barnabas spoke to his men in his own language, and now they formed a narrow circle round us under the pretence of being able to hear better. Still we expected no danger or treachery, because, although there was a rumour that the natives had arms and ammunition concealed in their houses, we knew that patrols of two and four had already passed there before

64. 'Lieuts. Muller and O'Reilly, Free State Artillery, who are still fighting in the Colony.' The photograph, which shows two members of a Free State commando with their black after-rider, was taken at Van Rhynsdorp on 19 January 1901, shortly after the invasion of the Cape Colony began. (Cape Times Weekly, 26.6.1901)

unharmed, and why should and how could they venture unarmed, as we considered them to be, to attack armed men?

To come to my story again, however. The General repeated his assuring words to them and asked them to listen to the proclamation. But now various questions, some of them insolent, began to be asked, the chief questioner being Barnabas. He asked the General point-blank whence he came and what he wanted here in their land, as they were British subjects. Genl. Maritz in return told him that it was time of war and he ought not to ask such questions. For a time he got them to order, and the proclamation was read and explained.

The General all the while kept cool and, as his custom is, spoke in the kindest and most complacent terms. But see, while the General was yet explaining the proclamation to them, Barnabas lifted his 'kerrie' and struck him over the head with the words, 'Watter rech het jij hier?', i.e., What right have you here? This was, of course, the sign for a general attack, for now the eager listeners, about forty in number, stormed down upon us. Barnabas was chiefly concerned with the General, whom he kept on hitting with the kerrie. The General, however, shouted to his men, 'Take your guns and fire', and himself tried to get one.

Now we must inform the reader that our horses stood loose at the side of the church, and we stood in front of them when this confusion and firing began. The horses therefore stampeded. They carried a rifle with them, and only two horses were kept.

But now the General had, when he got a gun in his hands, struck Barnabas over the neck, which blow brought him to the ground. Then he shot him through the side of his forehead. His men were also tackled, all of them, and when he had fought himself loose, he saw next to him one of his men wrestling with six natives, trying hard to keep his gun. He now ran to his assistance and shot two of them down. They, seeing their comrades falling down, fled into the houses and behind the walls, and now the armed men rushed forward, but luckily the General shot down the first, and this made them turn back.

The horses which were kept now were mounted to go after the other two horses. The General himself and the other men who had remained behind now also thought it safer to seek cover in the 'koppies', for as soon as the attack was made some of the armed natives had gone into the 'koppies' in order to cut off our retreat. The koppies being reached, we were safe – of course we still had to fire a shot now and again to keep them back, but they never ventured to come near to us. Thus we went forward until we reached our horses. Some of them were not caught, consequently some of us had to mount two on one horse.

We now went a little further to a good position, where we waited for them, but they did not pursue us any further, and we went back to Korenlandskloof.

According to our estimate there were about thirty armed men, some with Lee Metfords.

Here, of course, ends the story of the treachery of Lilyfountain. I may, however, add that one of our men had hurried out of Lilyfountain and gone to Comdt Kampfer's laager for reinforcements. This arrived at Korenlandskloof about half an hour after we came there. A report was sent to Comdt Schoeman that night informing him of what had happened, and telling him to attack them the next morning from Korenlandskloof.

Early the next morning this was done. We had expected they might have fled that night, but no, they were determined to defend their homes and lives to the bitter end against an enemy who, as their English friends had told them, came to annihilate them and to enslave their remains. It was found that they had taken position in the surrounding kopjes, and there they defended themselves to the end, not knowing of surrender at all.

When we came in the location we heard from the women that the preceding day eight were killed, and found that on the morning of the attack twenty-two were killed, besides some [who] were wounded in both instances. The women and children, with their wounded, were sent to Garies.

In conclusion I must add a few words in refutation to the malicious slanders and lies which, as the custom is from long years, are and have already been spread among some. Although we discovered from the diaries of the Missionary that he

131

65. 'The Kamiesberg Mission as it appeared in 1903. The picture shows the present school buildings with the church and mission house adjoining.' (From, Thomas Cheeseman: The Story of William Threlfall (1910))

was not only against us with his sympathy, but had actually taken up arms against us, we did not in the least wilfully destroy his piano and books or any articles of his. Of course we took what we required, but nothing more.

No single house or any other thing was burned, only the corn was taken which was found in the place and to whose possession we were fully justified.

'Reacting violently, as he usually did when he found Coloureds supporting the British cause, M[aritz] returned the following day and ruthlessly wiped out the settlement', remarks the Dictionary of South African Biography on the events at Leliefontein.

As mentioned in the account given above, the resident missionary, J.G. Locke, was not present at the time of Maritz's visit. With regard to the 'malicious slanders and lies' spread about the conduct of the Boers, one may note that on 14 June, after revisiting his mission, he addressed a letter to the Methodist Churchman in which he wrote about his house: 'My private correspondence lay scattered about the floors and mixed up with broken lamps, damaged books, papers, spoilt photographs, smashed window-panes, prickly-pear peels, bits of piano and other furniture, broken ornaments, indescribable filth – the whole spattered with black and red ink by way of ornamentation!'

It was in reply to the reaction caused by this that Locke received the following letter:

66. 'A group of Namaquas', a photograph taken at Leliefontein by A. Withinshaw and published in 1910. The men are identified as (front row): Jacob Jagers, 'the late Barnabas Shaw Links (brother of Jacob Links)', and Jan Kriel; and (back row): Frederick Smit, John Dirk, Peter Links and Johannes Boyse. (From, Thomas Cheeseman: The Story of William Threlfall (1910))

the author was probably a son of D.J. Malan, a general dealer whose address is known to have been Victoria House, Wellington. The book referred to would seem rather curious reading matter for a burgher on commando: while it may well have been an edifying work, it is tempting to speculate that it was of a more frivolous or worldly nature, and that Malan's letter was in fact meant to be facetious.

Victoria House, Wellington, 2nd Sept. 1902

Dear Revd Gentleman, – Your book *Woman: Her Charm and Power* was removed from your study library by one of our Burgers during our stay at Leliefontein. Perchance the book came into my hand, and [I] studied it with great blessing and much pleasure. Would gladly have returned the same to you with thanks, but unfortunately it was spoiled on commando. With a heart filled with joy and thanks, however, I beg leave to ask you to accept the accompanying Post Office order as a recompense for the loss sustained, from your humble, P. Jacs Malan.

67. 'Natives awaiting rations in Griquatown', from a newspaper photograph of the time. As a result of the Boer invasion, martial law was proclaimed throughout the Cape Colony and the civilian population involved in violence and disruption which were to last for eighteen months. (Cape Times Weekly, 15.1.1902)

Locke's papers relating to the war in Namaqualand were preserved in the archives of the Methodist Book Room in Cape Town, and now form part of the Methodist Church Collection at the South African Library. They support the view in the anonymous account quoted above that he was 'against us with his sympathy' and had given active assistance to the British military authorities, as was no more than his duty.

As guerrilla activities in Namaqualand intensified, Locke had probably retired for greater security to the small mining town of Okiep, where he thus found himself when it was suddenly besieged by Smuts on 4 April 1902. Among his surviving papers is part of his diary covering the latter part of the siege: the extracts given below begin towards the end of the month. According to The Times History of the War *the siege soon 'degenerated into a mere blockade, conducted with so much mutual good humour that on one occasion a challenge to a football match was carefully considered by the garrison and eventually declined.' It is understandable that Locke, who had been faced with the daily realities of war for well over a year and was well aware of what it meant for his mission, was less inclined to be good-humoured about the matter in his diary. The account was probably written for his wife, and 'Quillums' may be presumed to be their child.*

29.4.0[2]. Peculiar things happen sometimes even in war. The enemy who have done their best to kill us, including women and children, were anxious to play a game of football with a team from our Garrison this afternoon. Many of us are indignant that some of our officers are quite prepared to meet their wishes, and if consent is given by

68. *A photograph taken after an attack by the Boers on the Free State village of Philippolis in October 1900.* The Times History of the War *mentioned its 'plucky' defence by 'a little band of 18 British residents, 11 police and 12 Afrikanders', the latter referring to the coloured members of the local town guard shown here. 'These Kaffirs bravely took their part in the defence', stated the original caption.* (Cape Times Weekly, 26.12.1900)

Col. Cooper they will play. Such trifling under personal circumstances is to my mind totally uncalled for. Let us finish the war first, and then perhaps we shall be ready to meet the Boer in such friendly contests. Maritz himself is prepared to Captain the Boer team. He is one of the strongest men physically in the country.

My own idea is that the wily Boer desires to maim as many of our men as possible on the field, seeing that he is not very successful in the Game of Strife[?]. If they could disable an officer or two, how they would rejoice and laugh at the gullibility of the English. We sincerely hope Col. Cooper will helio an emphatic *No*.

What will Col. Cooper say? We send an urgent request for reinforcements, and when they are fighting their way to us and losing men in battle, lo! we send and ask for permission to play football with the enemy in our vicinity! We deserve to be left to our own resources.

We have had a little too much of the white flag lately. First a request for two children – granted. Then a request for two ladies – disallowed. Then letters from Smuts asking us for the sake of humanity to remove our women and children to some place within our lines! Now *Maritz* comes in daylight near to Fort Shelton under the white flag with the ostensible motive of challenging our men to football. When will the Briton learn to know the Boer? I guarantee Maritz has a better idea of our stronghold, Fort Shelton, at this moment than he ever had before, for has he not been close to it in daylight?

Capt. Lutwick of the Warwicks was wounded this afternoon. It is most unfortunate, for he is a very capable officer and was in charge of the three blockhouses, Range, King Edward and Springbok Road. He is still very young, and married just before he left England. I hope the wound will not prove mortal.

It is rumoured that Garies is relieved. If true, then probably Col. White will reach us before Col. Cooper – if so we shall rejoice.

Capt. Freeland made his [*word illegible*] work hard this evening, and we trust with good effect. Some of the shells fell in beautiful position.

Col. Cooper did not deign to reply to helio asking for advice re football match. I am not at all surprised, and will not wonder if some one suffers by and bye. (*Note*: Col. Cooper did send a reply to the effect that the exigencies of the times did not allow of football.)

30.4.02. I believe the vanguard of the Relief Column has had to retreat and wait for reinforcements owing to the strength of the enemy opposing the advance. This means that unless the Southern Column is moving towards us rapidly, relief will be delayed for a time.

The Boers are busy, and using dynamite to some purpose blowing up culverts. This morning there was a big explosion beyond the mountain in the direction of Narrap. It is supposed that the enemy have blown up the engine and mining plant at the mine there. A dense volume of smoke rose heavenwards a few moments after the report. As I write, our shells are hissing through the air immediately overhead in the direction of the explosion, seeking revenge among the kopjes.

One month of the siege is almost over. As regards provisions, we are prepared for two more, but as regards inconvenience I think all are longing for the end. For my part I am now quite used to it – my only longing is for you and Quillums.

Okiep was in fact relieved only a few days later, on 3 May; but by that time the war itself was virtually over.

69. (opposite). '*Boer prisoners of war leaving Simon's Town camp for their homes*', a photograph by J. Boyer taken after the end of the war (detail). (Cape Times Weekly, 10.9.1902)

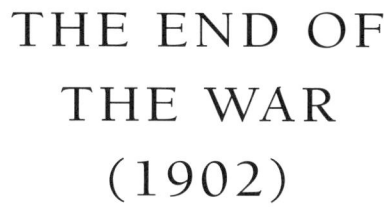

THE END OF
THE WAR
(1902)

*A*s the war entered its second year, public enthusiasm waned and interest in the protracted struggle diminished. What had started as a succession of dramatic battles
and campaigns had dwindled into a seemingly endless series of raids, skirmishes and
minor victories extending over the greater part of South Africa. By the end of 1901 it is
likely that most people wanted it all over and done with as soon as possible.

There were a few, however, who still felt strongly enough about the practice and principles
of the war to take a public stand, and among them, somewhat unexpectedly, was
Algernon Charles Swinburne. The sensual and glittering young poet of the 1860s and
1870s been left far behind, and at 64, Swinburne was installed in somewhat drab
domesticity in a London surburb. He was obviously in touch with the events of the day,
however, and specifically concerned about developments in South Africa, and this elicited
a letter from the Chief Justice of the Cape, Sir Henry de Villiers. Swinburne's reply has
been preserved among De Villiers's papers at the South African Library.

Sir Henry, later to become Lord de Villiers, was born Jacob Hendrik de Villiers, member
of an old Afrikaans-speaking Paarl family, and in spite of subsequent anglicisation and the
delicacy of his official position he seems to have felt obliged to comment on certain criticisms
on the Boers Swinburne had made in a letter to the Saturday Review. The nature of these
criticisms appears from Swinburne's reply, and it is worth noting especially his concern for
the 'dark races of South Africa'. Whatever the validity of the points he raised and the
reliability of his information, the concern itself must be appreciated. As has already been
noted with regard to Ettie Stakesby Lewis (see pp. 21-22 above), there were few people
anywhere who gave more than a passing thought to the situation of the blacks in South
Africa, except when it happened to suit their own convenience.

The Pines, Putney Hill, [London] SW
Nov. 27, 1901

Sir, – I thank you for your letter, & believe it is well intended: but if the accounts
of the brutal conduct of the Boer women as well as men towards English women
& children when our countrymen were driven out of the Transvaal, which
appeared in all the newspapers at the time, were ever refuted, the refutation never
came under my notice, although I have been a pretty careful reader of the news
from South Africa for the last two years. The pro-Boer press, except in the one case

of the *Westminster Gazette*, is so utterly & so unblushingly dishonest & disloyal that I could not accept any statement of fact on such notoriously worthless authority. If there had been in the one honest paper that can be called pro-Boer or Boerite such a refutation as you allude to of the charges brought on this occasion against the Boer women, I should certainly have been glad to read it.

In writing what I did I did not of course intend to suggest that all Boer women under all circustances were typical [of?] or fairly represented by those whose atrocities have been placed on record. To do so would have been to declare my own ignorance of general human nature. Shameful lies have been disseminated about my country-men & their cruelty towards women & children, & I in my defence of them adduced cases which the press had made notorious of the monstrous cruelty of the Boers towards English women & children. You say that there were no such cruelties, & I should like to think you were right: but at this very moment there are letters lying before me from writers who take a very different view from yours, men entitled to speak with great authority on the subject.

As to the cruelty of the Boers towards the dark races of South Africa, I have only to recall what Livingstone, Moffat & Colenso have said upon that subject to feel assured that the Scriptural studies of these devout Dutchmen can only have forti-fied & hardened them in the commission of atrocities which they need but power and opportunity to commit again. In the discussion of these matters I am disgusted rather than surprised at the deliberate & callous indifference of the Boerites with regard to the rights of the native races. Surely such Englishmen as those I have just named must have had some cause for their detestation of these born slavers & oppressors of races whose colour is their only crime.

As I have said in my letter to the *Saturday Review*, it seems to me that humanity has just escaped the disgrace of a hideous tragedy, when by the conquest & redemption of the Transvaal from systematic 'methods of barbarism' the back was broken of a cruel oligarchy which would have set its yoke on the neck of all the dark peoples from Cape Town to the Zambesi.

Believe me, dear Sir, yours faithfully, A.C. Swinburne.

The somewhat aimless feeling of the war dragging on is well reflected in an interesting document found without further information among the research materials of the late Eric Rosenthal. It is a typescript transcription headed 'Copy' and entitled, 'Private note book of Chris Liebenberg, Adjutant to General Liebenberg, operating in the district of Potchefstroom, Transvaal', and it covers the period 1 January to 9 April 1902. The com-mander in question was General P.J. Liebenberg of the Potchefstroom commando; Buisfontein which is mentioned in the excerpts below is some thirty kilometres to the north-west of Klerksdorp. Nothing more is known of Chris Liebenberg or the prove-nance of his journal, except that a few leaves of a photocopied manuscript also headed 'Copy' were found with the typescript. The text could well be a literal translation from a Dutch original, although it may equally reflect the author's limited command of English.

'This is my birthday', noted Liebenberg on 30 March. 'Oh, it is awful, much worse than last year.' While giving much information about life on commando, however, his journal is particularly good on the desolation of the countryside and the sufferings of the civilian population still remaining out in the field at this late stage of the war; four random entries reflecting this are given below. As mentioned here, Cecil Rhodes had died in Cape Town on 26 March.

Sunday, 5th [January 1902], [Buisfontein]. A very great change in the weather. It is as cold as in the heart of winter. We can hear cannon shots in the direction of Slypsteen. I was ordered to go and find out where the enemy is, but not being well was excused. The time in camp is very slow passing and not by any means pleasant.

Monday, 6th. I was busy in trying to get my horses shod. In the afternoon four of us left with the General to our farm, where some documents of his are buried, and now to be taken out again for secret purposes. My notes that have been hidden there are wanted too. When it was quite dark we reached the site where our house stood. After ten minutes I had my notes and the General his. Then I cast a searching look round the dear old farm; it was quite dark now, but I could distinctly view the damage that had been done. All houses, barns, kraals etc. have been broken down to the footing, and of our dwelling a few pieces of the inside wall about 5 feet high appeared above the ruins. You can imagine in what a sad melancholy mood I was thrown by the effect of the dear old place. After an hour's slow riding we were with the rest of our commando.

(. . .)

Saturday, 22nd [February]. Rain and nothing but rain. I went over to Paarde Plaats for some work. When there I made a round to the different sheltering places for the Free State families now residing there. Fever has made its visit to the poor wanderers and has only taken for its prey one young woman and several cases are very bad. It is indeed very touching and lamentable to see how hard their lot at present is. They must live on very little food and houses. Houses, I say. No, it would be right to say sheltering nooks, for the buildings on this farm (and in the whole district) were burnt down, some of which retain only one room under roof. In these nooks they reside. Very sad, I am sure you will say, and yet though fate is so cruel towards them, they remain full of courage and try to make themselves content.

(. . .)

Saturday, 5th [April]. We are now at Buisfontein on the hill where we took up our positions. Everything with us is quiet. We surmise that the enemy are the other side of Schoonspruit busy erecting a locomotive, and has also two engines which draw two iron trucks. The enemy has made great destruction here. Even the poor Kaffir they did not leave in peace. Some they took away, from others they burnt their food and destroyed furniture. I was informed that the following burghers were taken

70. 'Surrender of General Maritz's & other Boer commandoes at Kenhardt, 24.6.02'; no key has been provided to identify the numbered figures. Manie Maritz had been a prominent guerrilla leader in Namaqualand during the later phase of the war. (INIL 10955)

prisoner at G. kraal [sic]: J. Dassen and W. Liebbe. We and our horses are having a good rest. It is heartrending to leave our abodes and to see everything so desolate. I would not say anything, as it is a very sore point.

Some of the troops were informed by some of the women left behind that Rhodes died after a sickness of eight days.

Inexorably, however, the war was drawing to an end, and in his journal Liebenberg describes a formal visit from President Steyn and General de Wet on 18 March during which Steyn declared, 'The Lord can give us peace speedily, but it (the War) might last for years yet. But inwardly my spirit tells me that the end is not far off.' On 9 April representatives of the two Boer Governments met at Klerksdorp and decided to enter into negotiations with the British. On 15 May peace negotiations began at Vereeniging, and the end of the protracted war was already in sight by the time the relief of Okiep was celebrated with due ceremony.

J.B. Jardine of the Royal Irish Lancers, who in September 1899 had been in Pietermaritzburg, anxious to catch up with his Regiment lest he miss the war (see pp 10-12 above), had in fact missed nothing, and two and a half years later found himself in Namaqualand participating in what was, in effect, the end of the campaign in the west. In a letter to his mother shortly afterwards he could write, albeit with a 'certain amount of anxiety', about the peace negotiations which had already commenced at Vereeniging. General Smuts, who was operating in Namaqualand, had been brought to the conference via Cape Town; Sir Walter Hely Hutchinson was the Governor of the Cape in succession to Milner, who had become Administrator of the two Republics. Springbokfontein was the modern town of Springbok; Concordia itself had been taken by Smuts shortly before the siege of Okiep began.

Concordia, Namaqualand, 13th May 1902

Dearest Mother, – After reaching Ookiep we camped for three days outside the village, and on the third a grand (?) march past took place. This is the first time for three years that I have been in such a thing, but it was done to please the inhabitants and didn't hurt anyone. It was very mixed. Regular cavalry, regular Royal Artillery Yeomanry, irregular Royal Artillery, regular Infantry, Militia, black and tan Scouts, and Town Guard. Very funny.

After the parade we went on to Springbokfontein, but only stayed there two days, as the water was scarce, so came on here. The Boers have gone south, but have a strong post at Rietfontein S.E. of Ookiep to watch us. I don't know at present what is going to be done with us, but we all (the Column) hope to be sent away by sea back to Capetown. We are far too weak to go south by land via Garies, and I trust that French will take that view. I can't help thinking that French will not tolerate a weak column being outside his operations, and will bring us back. The 7th Fusiliers are already under orders to return and should start very soon.

This country is hideous and only fit for its aboriginal inhabitants. If you want to get an idea of it, get *Between Sun and Land* by W.C. Scully (Methuen & Co.). It is quite well written. We (Headquarters) are quite comfortable in a house at present, with drawing room, dining room, etc.; it belongs to a shopkeeper here who certainly has ideas of comfort. This is one of the men responsible for the surrender of the place, and a court-martial will be held on him shortly, I expect.

The Column is not two hundred strong now with two guns, not much of a command for Lieutenant Colonel. No word of officers or a draft coming out from home. I hear there are three or four hundred officers at Canterbury, and eight hundred men. And our squadron here is only seventy men strong on parade!

One hears little of the peace meetings. Great secrecy is kept regarding the whole affair. I imagine it is entirely between K. of K. and the Boeren, and that Milner has practically no say at all. Anyhow, when Barclay took Smutz to Cape town, Hely Hutchinson knew nothing about the matter. Smutz was not landed there, but went on to Simonstown, where the Admiral took charge of him and

71. 'Commandant de Villiers and his commando surrendering at the Kimberley diamond mine.' The reference is to P. J. de Villiers, who had been operating in Griqualand West; note the Indian men in turbans in the foreground, who were probably associated with the British forces. (Cape Times Weekly, 25.7.1902)

arranged about his railway journey. The civil authorities knowing so little gives colour to what I have said. Doubtless the Boeren prefer to consult direct with K. of K. and with him only. Delarey, I hear, is the most obstinate of them, and a man like Lucas Meyer has no authority whatever.

Smutz was very pro peace to all of us he met, but spies say he talked very differently in the Laagers. The opinion of a man like that will be greatly influenced by what K. of K. promises to do for him after the war. The rebel question has been overrated. The Transvaalers and Free Staters always speak of the Colonial[s] (Dutch or English of Cape Colony) with contempt for their fighting powers. I am not so pessimistic about prospects of peace as not to have a certain amount of anxiety about what the 15th will bring forth.

Best love to all, from your ever affectionate son, J.B. Jardine.

On 31 May 1902, however, peace was concluded, and suddenly everything was over and everyone could go home.

Among the very wide range of documents in the John X. Merriman Collection there is a fragment of two pages, part of a letter written, from internal evidence, by a

72. 'Comdt. Fouché returning to Cradock after promulgation of peace', another commercial photograph from the album of Lawrence Richardson; here too the shadow of the photographer with his camera has been recorded in the left foreground. W.F. Fouché had been active in the north-eastern Cape Colony during the guerrilla war. (INIL 10678)

Jagersfontein burgher held in a prisoner-of-war camp; it would seem to have been in South Africa, judging by the rather casual way in which his companions were leaving to return to their homes. T.K. Nieuwoudt and J.B.M. Hertzog were both guerrilla commanders from the Free State who had remained in the field to the end and had taken part in the negotiations at Vereeniging. [Translation on pp. 161-162.]

(...) den Dokter heb hem georderd om hier weg te gaan, het was my een zwaar slacht om Pa hier alleen te laten uitgaan, maar gy weet de tyd waarin wy leven zyn een *zeer kretieke*, men weet niet *wat* te doen en *wat* te laten, maar ik hoop spoedig te hooren wat my te doen staan.

Wy Jagersfonteiners wacht op tyding van Charlie Nieuwoudt of van Rechter Hertzog, hy zal toch natuurlyk aan zyn Broeder Koos schryf wat te doen. In alle geval wy zullen nu niet lang hier meer blyven, de menschen gaat veel uit, ik geloof gisteren en vandaag zyn er zoo wat 200 in getal uit, maar van morgen af zal hulle eerst begin uitgaan. Uit onze hut is van morgen twee, maar morgen zal er nog meer uit gaan.

Als Pa al daar is, zeg aan hem Sauer wou ook gister uit gaan, maar hy was laat, nu het hy weder zyn plan veranderd om nog te wacht.

Met my en Jaap gaat het nog eerste klas. Vandag laat ik weer een ontzaglyke pot ryst en melk kooken. Ik is weer generaal van onze Mess. Denk niet om my, ik heb goede maters, ons is vyf Vry Staters hier in die hut, verder alle Trans Valers. Ik is genooid om elken avond by ou Mr. Visser en Johan een kopje koffie en wat er nog (. . .)

Much the same note of impatience and uncertainty is to be heard in the diary of Mrs Schabort, who had been captured by the British in the north-eastern Free State the previous November (see pp. 88-90 above), and who at the end of the war found herself in the concentration camp at Merebank waiting for her husband to return from India. From the condition of the original document it would appear that she compiled the account of her capture in the camp, and that these final notes were added in the form of diary entries. [Translation on p. 162.]

Nu hebben wy tog de troost, al heeft wy nu alles verlooren zal wy tog nu spoedig uit die treurige kampen koomen en ons dierbaaren ontmoet van wien wy al zoo lang gescheiden ben, ook ons dierbaare die als krygsgevangenen weg gevoerd tereg [*sic*] te zien. Maar helaas, het is nu meer als een maand vrede en wy allen zit nog hier, ook van ons krygsgevangenen horen wy niets. Het schynt of Engelsman ons wil moor en uitroei zoo ver hulle kan, wy zitten nu al vedag ['*vandag*'?] twee dagen zonder zuiker, die arme kindertjies moet die tea uit die ketel drink en zwart daarby, daar wy van de morgen tot de avond by de koshuis moet staan in die bloedige zon en regen, en dan nog met die lege hande [*passage missing*].

3 July 1902. Nog zit wy met de verlangende harten om naar huis te gaan en ons dierbaarens terug te zien, maar er is onder geen omstandigheid gena ver de menschen, arme mans zit met verlangende harten daar buiten, stuur een telegram op de ander, de vrou moet koomen, maar dan is dit nog de kinder en dan weder iets anders.

Op 25 Augustus ben ik uit naar Bethlehem. Op 23 September ben myn echtgenoot terug gekoomen van India op eigen kosten, naar een ballingschap van 6 maanden. Op 9 October ben wy hier op onze plaats Glen Alphen aangekoomen.

The Schaborts and the nameless Jagersfontein burgher, together with tens of thousands of other South Africans, both black and white, returned to the devastation and desolation caused by almost two years of bitter guerrilla fighting. Even those people who had suffered no personal harm had to deal with the losses and violent disruptions caused by the war and the painful dissensions it had caused.

The surviving members of the British forces were luckier, for most of them returned home to a country untouched by war, where, with a little wishful thinking on the part of those who had been left behind, they were received as heroes and victors. R.B. Pott can perhaps speak on behalf of these men, for although his term of service was over by

73. 'Boers on the Parade at Jamestown listening to the Governor of St Helena explaining the peace terms.'
(Cape Times Weekly, 23.7.1902)

the middle of 1901, when the war in South Africa still had a year to go, the reception he received cannot have differed much from those accorded the soldiers who came back to England in the summer of 1902.

'Kentish fire', by dictionary definition, is 'a prolonged and ordered salvo or volley of applause'.

Friday, 19th July 1901. Disembarked and entrained at 8 a.m. Mills came with us. I tried to write speeches in the train and wished I had never been born.

Train arrived at Maidstone about 1 o'clock amidst the explosion of signals and much cheering. Platform crowded with many men in uniform who had been invalided home. Hamilton and Stanley also there, having brought Mother and the girls to the Star Hotel. Met by Colonel Warde. I fell in my men and marched them outside the station, where the Home Yeomanry were drawn up to receive us as well as the Mayor and Corporation. After a general salute, the order 'Busbies off, and three cheers for our comrades from the front.' This was followed by Kentish fire. Then the Mayor read an address, to which I replied.

We then marched to the parish church, where a thanksgiving service was held,

74. 'Peace!! Petrusville', a final snapshot from the albums of E.S. Barrett. The left-hand section of the building is a shop, but the signboard (behind the Union Jack) has been damaged and is no longer legible. A woman in a sun-bonnet and a man with a mourning band around his sleeve are among the people standing beside the scales. (INIL 2837)

and thence to the Corn Exchange, where we had luncheon. Colonel Warde gave the toast of the officers and men returned from South Africa, and coupled my name and that of Mills. I returned thanks, followed by Mills, who with his usual generosity refused to reply first.

At 8 o'clock in the evening I returned to Tunbridge Wells, and both there and at Southborough, where I was presented with and replied to another address, I received a most gratifying reception. Lord Henry Nevill and Macbean met me at Tunbridge Wells station. I was escorted by C Troop West Kent Yeomanry from Tunbridge Wells, and met at Southborough by brass band, fire brigade and hundreds of people, while the Sussex Voluntary Company and the Royal Engineers lined the roads. I was then escorted to Bentham Hill.

At 8 p.m. I arrived at home once more, after an absence of eighteen months. The Park was beautifully decorated, and all through Southborough triumphal arches were erected. I dined that evening with my family, the mother, sisters, Hamilton and his wife, Uncle Norbury, and Winifred, Rhoda and Florance.

Pott returned to a country home, a loving family, wealth, position and social security, but others were not so fortunate, and some members of the British forces preferred to stay on in South Africa after the war. Among them was James Bell, who seems to have considered his uncertain prospects in the new colonies more promising than the familiar situation in Glasgow. Two months after the end of the war he was still in Cape Town; from a street directory it appears that he was writing from the Alexandra Restaurant and Boarding House on the corner of Bree and Strand Streets, in an area where there were many small hotels and boarding houses. The coronation of Edward VII took place on 9 August and was celebrated with some ebullience by the victors; the feelings of the vanquished were probably mixed. The war being over, however, and bygones bygones, the Boer generals De Wet and De la Rey had been received with some enthusiasm when they passed through Cape Town on their way to Europe.

39 Bree Street, Cape Town, 4/8/02

Dear Father and Mother, – Just a few lines to let you know that I have been disbanded at last and am now a free man. I got Father's letter and am glad to hear that you are all well at home. I suppose you will have got your summer holidays over long ere this reaches you, and I hope you have enjoyed yourselves.

I am undecided what to do, go up country or stay here. I've got pretty fair views here, but am not sure further up, however, I'll write to let you know further.

Things are pretty lively here just now with all the troops coming down re-embarking for home. They are being sent away wholesale.

There are great preparations being made for the King's coronation day, and it will be a gay day here.

De la Ray and De Wet got a great reception in town last week by the Dutch element, and there is plenty here, they were dragged thro' the town by men.

I am in excellent health and hope that this finds you in the same.

Do not write any more letters to the Drill Hall, as I will forward you an address next week. This is all at present, so with kind regards, your affectionate son, James.

By the beginning of 1904 Bell was still in Cape Town. 'I am in good health,' he wrote to his father, 'and am working away as usual, but things are in a deplorable bad condition all over the country and there are thousands practically speaking starving. There is nothing further of importance to write about.' This is the last letter by him in the sequence, and it is not known what became of him afterwards.

75. (opposite). A snapshot taken by Lawrence Richardson on the station platform at Springfontein in October 1902 (detail). The local concentration camp was still in existence, five months after the end of the war, pending the return of prisoners of war from abroad and their resettlement on their devastated farms; the women shown here were probably inmates. In his diary Richardson mentioned seeing the 'neat rows of white tents' from the train. (INIL 10404)

TRANSLATIONS

The following translations have been kept as close to the style of the Dutch originals as feasible: only one of the writers concerned, Jacoba Lorentz, was Dutch by birth, and all the others show visible signs of uneasiness with the medium, while some were obviously barely literate.

In the translations, the names of people and places referred to have been given in the correct spelling, as far as this could be established. Explanatory footnotes, where required, have been given here with the translations rather than in the body of the book with the original Dutch texts, but general introductions will be found with the texts themselves.

p. 17, D.J. Viljoen to W.P. Schreiner

Stuurmans River, 11 Oct. 1899

The Hon. W.P. Schreiner, Prime Minister

Sir, – Received Your Honour's telegram. I am delighted that I have already been active in this spirit. Feelings are very excited, but up to now I have met no-one who could be accused of disloyalty.

All are loyal solely to the Crown, but all abominate the Capitalist Clique whose politics are now being carried out by the Imperial Government.

We regret very much that Imperial troops are being placed here among us, and who then appear to believe that they can do as they like on private property.

Sir, we are *loyal*, but believe me our hearts are bleeding and our eyes weep over our brethren in the Republics who are being dragged into an unjust war.

I remain, Sir, Your Honour's humble servant, D.J. Viljoen.

p. 52, Jacoba Lorentz on the British occupation of Pretoria

Pretoria, 6 June 1900

Dear Trui, – The die has finally been cast, and we are English. Yesterday 50 000 soldiers entered the town and took possession of it. Luckily everything went off in a very peaceful and orderly manner. The troops did not display their joy in looks or gestures, and behaved in a most modest and considerate way wherever they came in contact with the public. This is what was to be expected of a civilised nation, but there had been so many dreadful stories in the papers about the misconduct of the soldiers, especially in respect of women, that we were fearful about their arrival, and many women had armed themselves for defence, in the absence of the men, against an excited and savage horde, as the soldiers had been represented to us. Fortunately everything went off in excellent order. In a quiet and disciplined manner they filled the streets and marched across Church Square. Lord Roberts also entered the town quite unnoticed, and no music or signs of joy offensive to our feelings were to be heard or seen, and it was late in the day before the English flag was raised over the Government buildings. This is a thorn in my flesh, more than I can express. The war is completely unjust, and the English have simply robbed us of what is ours; there is no other explanation for this annexation. And when one thinks about it, one feels rebellious about such great injustice. How can God allow injustice to triumph in this way? we have cried repeatedly during the past months. The actions of the English cry out to heaven and demand vengeance. (. . .)

p. 76, P.A. Geldenhuis to his wife

Green Point, 8/1/1901

Dear and beloved wife, – By the goodness of God we are all still reasonably well and wish you all the same. Dear wife, it is now some time since I last heard from you, I have heard about various families having been sent away, so that I am very curious about what has happened to you.

Brother-in-law Machiel and Frederik and Cornelis Taljaard are still with me, also Stoffels Nagel, the other acquaintances have almost all been sent away. Papa and Matthys Taljaard have arrived in Ceylon. I have received a letter from brother Mathys from St Helena dated 13 Dec., he was then still well.

I feel as healthy now as when I was just married, I have a cold bath every morning now and it is of great benefit to me. It is a pity that I have to see the sea water every day and cannot bathe in it. About our food and drink I can't complain.

As far as the spiritual life is concerned, everything is going very well under the circumstances, we have a service here every day, at first it was led by Dominee du Toit and by Dominee Alheit, he once preached to us at Heilbron. Mr Spreth also preaches to us, and he does it very well. A week ago more than 400 children were confirmed, among them was P.A. Badenhorst. Cornelis Taljaard was ill at the time, an abscess in his ear, otherwise he would have finished too. He is studying well again.

Jan Scheepers, Oom Lukas's son, is here too, if you can you must let his wife know that they are still well.

So I remain with affectionate greetings and blessings, your husband, P.A. Geldenhuis.

151

You must write out my name in full on my address. When you write then it must be: Prisoner of war at Green Point, Camp No.1, C.C.

pp. 82-84, Dominee D.J. Viljoen on his arrival in India

Monday, 22 April [1901]. We had catechism instruction this morning. Afterwards our prayer meeting took place. Our principal thoughts were: gratitude that the Lord has led us safely over the great waters, and prayer that He may lead and preserve us in the unfamiliar India. In the afternoon the last petition of the Our Father was discussed.

Tuesday, 24 April. When we awoke Bombay was in sight. Towards one o'clock we steamed into the harbour. The heat was intense. The number of spectators was very large, and it would have been even larger if the ship had arrived the following day as expected. There was very great curiosity to see the Boer prisoners of war. And when they saw us they were disappointed. They had imagined us to be little men with long hair and untrimmed beards, while the Boers looked like every other European.

If the curiosity was great, the interest and the sympathy for us on various sides was even greater. No word of contempt was heard, and no sign of hatred or spite was to be seen. How different from Cape Town, where our poor prisoners of war were reviled in the streets as all that is ugly and ridiculous.

As we were not allowed to go into the town, we were unable to see anything of the place. At about 6:20 the first train left with part of the men and eleven officers. The remainder went on the second train. Before we left the burghers at the request of an English lady sang the two national anthems. It was striking to see with what respect the anthems were received by the many onlookers.

It was moonlight, so that we were at least able to see that we were passing through a very mountainous region. We went through no fewer than 26 tunnels. Although it was night, there were large crowds of curious and interested people at all the stations. We travelled very pleasantly, for as the officers were on parole, we did not have the inevitable soldier with us.[1] It was accordingly very late at night before we fell asleep.

Wednesday, 24 April. When we awoke this morning we were very disappointed. Everything looked very dry, as it has not rained properly for a long time. Here and there we saw small flocks of goats, at one place a few antelopes. Apart from that only Indians with two or four oxen harnessed to their ploughs, busy scratching at the dry earth (one can't call it ploughing) in the hope that the indispensable rain will follow.

By seven o'clock in the morning we arrived at the station of Ahmednagar. The

---

1. *i.e., an armed British guard.*

distance from the station to the camp is about 4 miles. We had of course to go on foot, and after about an hour's walk we arrived at the fort. When we saw the high walls we felt anything but comfortable. Strangers in a strange land, and on top of that shut up in a kind of 'tronk' (prison). We were no less downcast once we were inside the fort. Everything looked very mournful. Hardly a green leaf, the heat unbearable, locked up between high walls, and in addition barbed wire and the inevitable armed men around us. We could not help thinking: We shall not be here long before a large number of us will have found their graves in a foreign country. It must be added here that our fears subsequently proved unfounded, for during all this time we lost only ten prisoners.

After our arrival we were counted, and then it was discovered that one of the prisoners had escaped. He was called Grey. What happened to him we were unable to discover. This incident caused us much discomfort, as we were counted repeatedly.

The prisoners of war took up their quarters in *bungalos* [sic] or corrugated iron huts. It need hardly be said that we were all very tired and that we spent the greatest part of the day sleeping.

pp. 84-85, B.A. and A.W. Lourens to W.J. Uys

Heidelberg [Tvl.], the 20 October 1900

Dear old brother W.J. Uys, prisoner of war at Green Point, – Your dear letter found us well. We still find ourselves in the hour of grace, although with much distress of body, and also the circumstances of the times have cast us down to the earth, life is bitter to us. Never did we think that we would in our old age be reduced to such a condition as that in which we now find ourselves. The people ask where is thy God?[1] Dear brother, for more than a year we have received no news of any relative or children, no letter, in reply to your note to Uys I sent two letters to you in Kroonstad, now we have received four letters at a time, one from Jan Eksteen in gaol in Newcastle, one from Michiel, he has been prisoner of war on board ship in Natal for more than a month, and now I have received your letter telling me that you and your dear children are also prisoners of war at Green Point, and this is too much for us to bear for an old man. Brother, what is there I can do for you, can't I stand surety for you, then I will look after you if necessary. Find out from the authorities. It is your old sister I feel sorry for.

Our life goes by with sighs and prayers, many of our dear ones have passed away, such as brother Hans Uys, Waterkloof, and C. Uys, Maskloof, and many others besides. [What happened to Miss Susara after she left home?][2] How is your health

1. *A scriptural quotation (Psalm 42).*
2. *Translation conjectural.*

in the camp? Is Piet Geldenhuis alive? Tell him I want a letter from him.

We greet all your children and yourself with a loving kiss. May the Lord be close to you and yours, may He let the light of His countenance shine upon you, may He have mercy on you, may He let the light of His countenance shine upon you, may He have mercy on you, is the prayer of your brother and sister, B.A. and A.W. Lourens.

P.S. Katie and Ben have just arrived here, and Francis is here too with her cart. Your dear sister asks whether she can't send you a bible. If I knew that our Government would allow me to see you and the others, I would come. Poor Giel has asked me for money, but I don't know how to get it to him.

pp. 85-86, F. Geldenhuis to her husband

Honingspruit, 25th March 1901

Dear and beloved husband, – With joy I have received your letter of the 12th March in which you ask me for a little money. Our good friend has sent you five pounds. I hope that you have received it already.

Everything is going very well with us, we have nothing to complain of, everything [is] plentiful. It is raining well here, almost every day. Hennie can talk well, only full of mischief. [I have much trouble with Ma, is heavy and uncomfortable.][1]

You say I must write to you every week. My right arm hurts and the trembling in my arm is so bad that writing is very troublesome for me. [All this caused by the heavy body I have to rule.][2] I will do what I can.

All the rest of the family are well. Give my greetings to everyone I know, also to brother Frederik. Write me where he is. Give my greetings to Papa and to all the brothers when you write to them again. I last wrote to you in February.

I sign myself your wife, greet you with a loving kiss, F. Geldenhuis.

pp.88-90, A.S. Schabort on her removal to a concentration camp

On Thursday, 7 November [1901] we had to take leave of our loved ones who then had to seek safety for their cattle again. We, however, Aunt Cornelia Buys and children, Martje Boshoff and I with my children and a little black boy, then remained behind on the farm of Michiel Uys, Kalverspruit, where we had been told that our civilised foe would no longer capture women and children.

Then a patrol[3] arrived from Standerton, they passed close by us and pitched

1. *Meaning unclear; but see the following note.*
2. *Meaning unclear; but possibly to be read in conjunction with the previous conjectural passage.*
3. *'camp' throughout in the original.*

camp about 1/2 hour on horseback from us, their spies approached close to us and turned back again. The patrol remained in camp behind Tafelkop for two or three days. Oh, we experienced bitter days, not a night or day did we have rest, for we were always expecting the enemy at any moment, and we knew that nothing was too good for them.[1] We kept looking out for them carefully from a ridge immediately behind the house.

At last came the happy news, the enemy has gone off in the direction of Frankfort. Oh how glad we then were to think that we had escaped without the bitter [necessity of] flight, for the first man who arrived, Frans v.d. Berg, assured us that they had all passed through the Wilge River and that there were ten patrols out in that direction. Oh how distressed we then were once more about our men and cattle, not knowing what had become of them, but finally we thought that if the Lord would only help our husbands and children through safely, even though the cattle were lost.

Now we sat waiting with anxious hearts for news of our dear ones. At last T.B. arrived late on the 13 November, at or after sunset, we immediately recognised the horses at quite a distance, but we felt very bad, for we knew that one of them had drawn my cart and we thought that everything had been lost, but then we all had to hear how bitterly they had passed through those patrols and had to leave behind all the carts, not knowing what had happened to them, also not knowing what had happened to our people that morning after T.B. had left them, for he had hardly left when a troop arrived at the same place, I think it was De Lange's Drift. Yes, we felt the lot of our loved ones deeply, but what was awaiting us?

The patrol was at that time established at a distance of an hour or more from us, on Albertus van Wyk's farm, near Leeuwkop, but [coming?] straight in our direction. We spent a bitter night, I could not settle down before I had cast in my lot with God. Let come what may, I am under God's hand and guidance.

T.B. left us that evening to seek a safe place for himself and my two cows which had then been sent out in the care of the little black boy until he could reach them to tell them in what direction [to go]. I was very worried that night about T.B. in case he might be very tired and oversleep the next day instead of reconnoitring in what direction the cows should go.

The following day we were out of bed very early when it was still half dark in order to see what the Dragon's intentions might be,[2] and then also to put on our clothes as far as possible one article over the other, as he, the Dragon, was in the habit of burning everything and leaving you with only the clothes you were wearing, without food or clothing or bedding.

Then we saw him coming, with great fear as to what would become of us, the

---

1. *Possibly in the sense, 'anything might expected of them'.*
2. *'Draake' in the original – 'dragon' or 'beast', apparently referring to the British, probably with scriptural connotations (see Revelations 7).*

whole patrol came down upon us, rather, the first lot came, were very unfriendly, for we heard them shooting something to kill it, it must have been a dog or a calf. We pretended not to understand, in order to find out what was happening. There was an old coloured man there who said, You must get ready, the patrol will probably[1] take you away, we've got a whole lot of women; but then we were deeply cast down to think that our parting might possibly be for ever without our having realised it, but we thought we would still get off through the crippled son of 14 years old of Stoffel Botha.

Now the second lot under Allison arrived. As soon as he saw me he said, Your husband came to surrender yesterday.[2] Then I said, I don't have such a coward of a husband. Then he asked, Aren't you Mrs T.B.? I said, No. [Then our old friend M. was standing there in the room laughing. What was the matter? T. thought he had never told me anything about it, imagined everything to have been pre-arranged, for they were almost always alone together that afternoon.][3] When I told Allison so, All right then, get ready quickly, T.B. says you must come. No, we don't feel like coming, and look at the poor crippled child. The doctor was soon there, but no mercy, we had to be quick, the wagon was on its way. Then all the things we had hidden away for so long were tracked down by the dirty hands-uppers and armed blacks, of whom there were many. Yes, everything was broken and spoiled, and they took away as much as they could for their poor naked families.

pp. 91-94, Jacoba Lorentz on the concentration camp at Arcadia

23 July [1901]. This morning I again visited the women's camp at Arcadia. Many tents were empty, and I was told that a large number of women had again been taken to Irene.

In a tent I entered I found a girl of 11 years ill with pneumonia. She appeared to me to be on the point of death. The mother, Mrs Coetzee, told me that they had been brought in from Schurfteberg recently, that the child had been complaining of pain in the chest for months already, that they had on the way here had to sleep in the open for three nights, although it was bitingly cold and freezing, and that the child had then caught a cold. She had been ill for a week already. Dr van Wijk had been called in three days ago and had supplied medicines for her, which the mother was not giving her any more, as they had made the child feel as if she were suffocating. There she accordingly lay in delirium, and no-one knew what to do. The mother simply sat looking on with dry eyes in silent despair.

I went in to town and happened to find the doctor in his pharmacy. He was

1. Or 'certainly'; the meaning of 'seker' (possibly 'vir seker') is not clear.
2. The English 'serender' has been used in the original.
3. The punctuation and meaning of the passage between square brackets is not clear in the original.

immediately prepared to go to the camp and at least give good advice as to further treatment if the mother should persist in refusing to administer the medicines.

A short while ago I heard that the poor child was dead, and also that the relatives of the President who were still in Pretoria have been ordered to leave the country. Today it was further rumoured that the military administration intends to expel all women whose husbands are still on commando from the country.

25 July. This morning I again visited the women's camp to take sheets and Bovril to Mrs Kleynhans, who has three children ill with measles. All three of them were lying of a chest over which a few blankets had been spread. I advised her to sponge the children with lukewarm water, as they were quite black with dust and grime.

I next made my way to the tent of Mrs Coetzee, the woman whose daughter died the day before yesterday. The funeral had not yet taken place, as the doctor had not yet been able to send in the death certificate, having been too occupied. While I stood talking to the woman at the entrance to her tent, she said suddenly: 'There's the little hearse.' The poor woman barely had time to realise the implications of this for her. A small child was crying uninterruptedly and needed attention. Two other children, a girl of 13 and a boy of 7, were lying ill in bed. A boy of 14 was dressed in new clothes with a mourning band around his hat, and would be the only mourner following the little corpse.

The hearse stopped in front of the tent, and immediately a number of Boers, women and children, gathered at the entrance. An elderly man asked us to sing Ps. 103:8, 'Our brief life is like the grass,/ Like a flower in the field', etc., etc. At first there was no one who could intone, but at last a young Boer woman, assisted by a friend, began singing in a harsh, dragging tone, after which we all joined in.

It was a motley crowd of men, women and small children, most of them dressed in typically Boer fashion, and of all ages. Opposite me stood an old man with a red neckerchief the ends of which hung down his back, bowed, and with his hair falling down from to all sides from the crown of his head in typical Huguenot fashion, who transported me in my thoughts to the time of the Covenanters.[1] Beyond him my eyes dwelled on the river and on the Magaliesberg in the blue distance.

When we had finished singing the verse, the precentor prayed. He thanked God that where the messenger of death had appeared in our midst, we were able to consign the deceased to her last resting place, while so many friends and relations were entering into eternity in these times without their nearest relatives knowing where they were lying. He also gave thanks for the fact that through this death we were reminded of our own, which was imminent. He prayed for the mother who had been obliged to give up her child, but for whom it was a consolation to know that her daughter had gone to Him who had said: 'Suffer little children to come unto me', etc.

---

1. In Dutch, *'de tijd der hagepreeken'*, *referring to the persecution of the Protestants during the Reformation.*

When the prayer ended, he informed us that the authorities only allowed *ten* minutes for the burial service; he could therefore neither read from the Bible nor make a speech. He only said that no matter how much we loved one another, so much that we were unable to part, that even though the mother pressed her child to her heart and would not let go of it, when death came she was obliged to let it go alone, thither no-one accompanies us. He then asked us to sing again, Hymn 20:8 and 9, 'When we enter the valley of death, / All earthly friends forsake us,' etc. And, 'Come, let us set forth with new heart,' etc. To the mother he said finally that she might say with David, 'She will not return to me, but I shall go to her.'

Thereupon a number of young men took up the little coffin, placed it in the hearse, and all went their various ways. Slowly the vehicle descended the slope towards the river, followed by a single mourner, the dead girl's fourteen-year-old brother.

pp. 94-96, Jacoba Lorentz on the funeral of Mrs Kruger

22 July [1901]. The day before yesterday Mrs Kruger, wife of the President, died. She was an invalid, and so obese that she never walked, but had to be driven even the shortest distances. For a number of years already she had had herself driven to church, which is across the street from her house. More recently she suffered greatly from the distress caused by the war to the country and the people, and in her own family she likewise had much cause for sorrow: the President away a year already, a son and his wife leading immoral lives, and several of her closest relatives fallen in battle or dead as a result of the war, also a number of her children and grand-children. She was a simple, amiable woman, a true Christian, who in the midst of all the worldliness surrounding her remained as far as possible true to the old-fashioned Boer way of life, and who therefore steadfastly refused to meet the Governor or any of the high-ranking English officers, saying that she was just a humble woman and did not know how to behave towards such people. She was worshipped by her children and grandchildren, approximately eighty in number.

Last week she fell ill with pneumonia, as happens frequently at this time of year when the dust is lying inches deep on the ground, but the immediate cause of her death was heart failure. It is a great loss for the President, but for her it is a release, she was much distressed by the situation and unable to cope with it.

Yesterday (Sunday) afternoon at three o'clock the funeral took place. I attended with someone I know. The carriage had to stop at a considerable distance from the house. The street was black with people and vehicles. There was a great crush, and it was only with difficulty that we managed to get into the house, swarms of people everywhere. We entered a big room and found the coffin there, covered with wreaths and guarded by a number of Boers. The coffin was of polished oak; a metal plate bore her name and age, 67 years, and wreaths covered the coffin and the floor around it. We saw no members of the family.

We next moved to another big room on the other side of the passage. A woman in black was sitting in the far corner weeping. From her appearance I judged her to be one of the President's daughters. Opposite her sat two women in the customary Boer costume with *kappies* and a third in ordinary clothes, all three of them in black. The woman wearing a hat and veil sat quoting scriptural texts in a loud voice and exhorting the weeping woman to resignation. It made an extraordinary impression, and reminded me of olden days when there were people in the colony with the title of Sick Comforters.

The bustle and throngs of people, the big room, in which a life-size portrait of the President was hanging and in which another Boer woman was also sitting at some distance wearing a *kappie* and one in modern dress, and the sorrow of the weeping woman who paid attention to nothing, but seemed to be listening to the woman who was speaking, the two other silent black figures with their backs partly towards me – I shall not easily forget the impression all this made on me.

When we could not find the members of the family for whom we were looking, we went outside again in the crowd and with great difficulty succeeded in reaching the church across the street, where a funeral service was to be held. The church was crowded. When we saw that there was no possibility of getting in, we went to the vestry, where there was more than enough room. I opened the door in order to be able to follow the sermon, and was given a chair by someone who got up for me. Dominee Bosman read a chapter from Revelations, and then took from the Book of Judges as text 'A Mother in Israel'. He spoke with great feeling on her merits as mother to her children, as mother to her people and as a Christian, emphasising the fact that she had been a sincere, simple, intensely devout Christian and one who was quiet in the land,[1] who had nonetheless exerted great influence. Finally he gave out from Psalm 25 the verse, 'Look down on me with favour from on high', changing 'me' to 'him' each time and thus making it applicable to the President. It was most moving to hear him read, 'Lonely is he and rejected,/ Yea, his sorrow bears him down,' etc.

Thereupon the cortège set off for the cemetery, a large part of the crowd following. And thus she is no more, she who since the President's departure had been the common bond uniting the people to one another. A sense of desolation overwhelms us when we think of the empty place, the empty house, which was for so long the centre uniting everything that would otherwise have fallen apart.

p. 122, C.J. Terblans to Thomas Searle

Mr Tom Searle, G.B.R. – A report has arrived here from Frumershum that Willem Willems and others of the other people, that they saw something there against the

---

1. *A scriptural allusion (Psalm 35:20).*

mountain about 2 miles from the Waterworks, it seemed to him like living things, and as it appeared from a distance it might have been about 30 men. I was not able to go and have a look, for it was dark, but I have ordered them to stand guard tonight, and to report immediately if they see anything. You can now think what can best be done further. C.J. Terblans, H.C.

pp. 123-124, Anonymous to Thomas Searle

[*place deleted*], 20.9.1901

To Tos. Searle, Esq., Brak River – Dear Sir, As you told me that our Commandant wants to know something about what the Boers said here at Kleinvallei about the war, I am most sure of what was said here was to me, for Cornelis was a prisoner, they told him not to leave his house, so I was better able to hear something.

What I am telling you you can take as the full truth, I shall not accuse the people falsely, but we must ask our Commandant not to use my name openly, as the people said that if we reported them they would burn down our farms and we might also expect other consequences.

As regards our conversation, after I had warned my children that we were not allowed to give the people anything, I went down to the old widow's house to give the people the same instructions. When I got there it was so dark, then I met a number of them in the farmyard. Then I told them they had placed us in a bad position by coming to make war in our colony, they surely could not hope to win victory with their weak force. Then one of them said that they now have more men than when the war started. Then one of them asked through what spectacles I was reading, whether I couldn't see that they were waging war out of England's pocket.[1]

I could not find out further whether their commandos know about each other, but one of them said they know everything happening in England. The rest of the conversation was of no importance.

Furthermore as far as I know any of the names, they are as follows: Commandant Theron, Lieutenant de Vos, Joubert, Lombaard, Boshoff, two Nels, O'Briens or something similar, Hildebrand, Louwrens.

1. *i.e., presumably, waging war at England's expense through commandeering, etc.*

160

A Dream

I, Anna Kloppers, 12 years old, dreamed at midnight that I came in by our middle door and I saw a very big man standing at the front door, a loose cloak hanging round his shoulders to his feet. On his forehead he wore a crown glittering with diamonds, in his hands he bore a burning pot and smoke came from it, white as white as snow, which rose straight up to heaven. On either side of the pot was a *Vierkleur* flag.

I then grew afraid. He noticed it and said, Do not fear. Then I called my mother. She asked him who he was. He said, I am Michael. She asked him where he was going. He said, I come from Ladysmith and am on my way to the Orange Free State. He said further, Do you see this pot, it is incense on the altar which I keep burning day and night, this oblation ensures victory to those who have suffered so much in Christ's name. The smoke was splendidly white like snow and it smelt wonderful. The smoke wasn't blowing about, but went straight up to heaven.

He said to my mother, read Psalm 110 from verse 5,[1] there you will see that this small nation will not be destroyed. Another text from the prophecies. The Lord is a strong refuge, etc. He will come with pestilence and they will know that I am the Lord.

Then my mother said, Come and rest a while, but he said, The birds of heaven have nests, but we have nowhere to lay our heads. I am the Alpha and Omega, this war has been begun, I shall also make an end to it, I have sworn it and this I shall do.

(. . .) the Doctor has ordered him to go away from here, it was a heavy blow to me to let Pa go out by himself, but you know that the times in which we are living are *very critical*, one doesn't know *what* to do and *what* to leave undone, but I hope to hear soon what I am to do.

We Jagersfontein men are waiting for news from Charlie Nieuwoudt or from Judge Hertzog, he will of course write to his brother Koos what to do. In any case, we shan't be staying here much longer, the people are leaving in great numbers, I believe yesterday and today about 200 left altogether, but as from tomorrow they will really begin leaving. From our hut two left this morning, but tomorrow there will be more.

If Pa is there already, tell him Sauer wanted to go out yesterday too, but he was late, now he has changed his plan again to wait a while still.

Everything is still first-class with me and Jaap. Today I'm having an enormous

---

1. *'The Lord at thy right hand shall strike through kings in the day of his wrath', etc*

pot of rice and milk cooked again. I'm General of our Mess again. Don't worry about me, I've got good mates, there are five of us Free Staters here in the hut, the rest are all Transvaalers. I have been invited to go over every evening to old Mr Visser and Johan for a cup of coffee and whatever (. . .)

p. 145, A.S. Schabort on the end of the war

Now at least we have the consolation although we have lost everything we will soon get out of the miserable camps and meet our loved ones from whom we have been separated for so long, also to see again our loved ones who were taken away as prisoners. But alas, it is already more than a month since the peace and we are all still sitting here, of our prisoners of war we hear nothing either. It seems as though the English want to kill and exterminate us as far as they can, today we have been without sugar for two days already, the poor little children have to drink the tea [as it comes?] from the kettle and black as well, as we have to stand at the food depot from morning to night in the blazing sun and rain, and then still [*passage missing*] with empty hands.

3 *July 1902*. We are still sitting with hearts yearning to return home and see our loved ones again, but there is no mercy for the people under any circumstances, poor men are sitting out there with yearning hearts, send one telegram after the other, the wife must come, but one moment it's the children and the next something else.

On 25 August I got out to Bethlehem. On 23 September my husband came back from India at his own expense, after an exile of 6 months. On 9 October we arrived here on our farm Glen Alphen.

SOURCES OF DOCUMENTS

The war begins (1899-1900)

p. 10, J.B. Jardine (Pietermaritzburg, 28.9.1899): J.B. Jardine Collection, MSB 272, 1(1) pp. 1-3.

p. 12, Sarah Leith (Grey College, Bloemfontein, 4.10.1899): Searle Collection, MSC 50, 6(5).

p. 14, Antonia Corelli Green (24.10.1899): Antonia Corelli Green Collection, MSB 218, 1(1).

p. 17, D.J. Viljoen (Stuurmans Rivier, 11.10.1899): W.P. Schreiner Collection, MSC 27, 1(61). Text of Schreiner's original telegram at MSC 27, 1(16). Text of Mostert's telegram at MSC 27, 1(62).

p. 18, Resident Magistrate, Dordrecht (27.11.1899): W.P. Schreiner Collection, MSC 27, 1(134).

p. 19, Secretary, Law Department, Cape Town (1.1.1900): W.P. Schreiner Collection, MSC 27, 2(171). Quotation from B.J. Jones from MSB 263, 1(1), pp. 185-186.

p. 21, The Picture Postcard Co. (London, 8.12.1899): W.P. Schreiner Collection, MSC 27, 1(154).

p. 21, Henrietta Stakesby Lewis (The Highlands, 28.1.1900): W.P. Schreiner Collection, MSC 27, 2 (211). Reply at MSC 27, 2(212). Quotation on Ettie Stakesby Lewis from S.C. Cronwright-Schreiner, *The Life of Olive Schreiner* (London: T. Fisher Unwin, 1924), p. 47.

p. 24, 'Tasmanian' (Hobart, 26.3.1900): W.P. Schreiner Collection, MSC 27, 2(286).

p. 26, Osmond Walrond (Government House, Cape Town, 4.4.1900): W.P. Schreiner Collection, MSC 27, 2(212). Newspaper report taken from 'The Premier', *Cape Argus Weekly* (4.4.1900), pp. 27-28.

THE SIEGES (1899-1900)

p. 28, M.W. Tyler (8.11.1899): M.W. Tyler Collection, MSB 496, 1(1).

p. 31, J.B. Jardine (22.12.1899): J.B. Jardine Collection, MSB 272, 1(1) pp. 42-44.

p. 32, Elizabeth Atkinson (Kimberley): Elizabeth Atkinson Collection, MSB 842, 1(1) pp. 1-2.

p. 36, Johanna Hendriksz (5.11.1899): Women's Studies Collection, MSB 892, 1(9), pp. 21-30. Telegrams relating to Johanna Hendriksz at MSB 18, 2(2).

p. 37, Elizabeth Atkinson (Kimberley): Elizabeth Atkinson Collection, MSB 842, 1(1) pp. 20-21, 23-24.

THE BRITISH ADVANCE (EARLY 1900)

p. 44, H.R. Langmore (6.12.1899): H.R. Langmore Collection, MSB 635, 1(1).

p. 47, J.B. Jardine (28.2.1900): J.B. Jardine Collection, MSB 272, 1(1).

p. 48, Maria Bamberger (6.3.1900): Maria Bamberger Collection, MSB 886, 1(1). Letter re A.N. Bamberger at MSC 8, 20(2) (23.10.1891).

p. 50, R.B. Pott (29.7.1900): R.B. Pott Collection, MSB 390, 1(1) pp. 112-117. Quotation on Brandwater surrender from *Times History* IV, 343.

p. 52, Jacoba Lorentz (Pretoria, 6.6.1900): Jacoba Lorentz Collection, MSB 964, 1(1).

p. 54, Percy Cogle (Edenburg, 16.4.1900): Percy Cogle Collection, MSB 644, 1(1).

p. 56, F.S. Barclay (Johannesburg, 8.6.1900): F.S. Barclay Collection, MSB 31, 1(1).

p. 61, Katie Stuart (Orange River battlefields): Earp Family Collection, MSC 47, 2(5), pp. 12-15. Quotation on Vigilance Committee from Karel Schoeman, *Only an Anguish to Live Here* (Cape Town: Human & Rousseau, 1992), p. 84.

SETTLING IN (LATE 1900)

p. 66, H.R. Langmore (6.8.1900): H.R. Langmore Collection, MSB 635, 1(1). Other extract quoted from entry for 21 July 1900.

p. 69, James Bell (Modder River Camp, 21.8.1900): James Bell Collection, MSB 593, 1(1). Quotation by Katie Stuart from MSC 47, 2(5).

p. 70, J.H. Kuhlmann (Pretoria, 12.9.1900): J.H. Kuhlmann Collection, MSB 285, 1(1).

p. 72, Maria Bamberger (24.12.1900): Maria Bamberger Collection, MSB 886, 1(1).

p. 73, B.J. Jones (6.7.1900): B.J. Jones Collection, MSB 263, 1(1), p. 21. Quotation on Mount Nelson from Sir Ralph Williams, *How I Became a Governor* (London: John Murray, 1913), p. 270.

THE VANQUISHED (1901)

p. 76, P.A. Geldenhuis (Groenepunt, 8.1.1901): H.C. Hopkins Collection, MSC 78, 12(18).

p. 78, P.J. de Beer (Green Point, 21.5.1901): Prisoner of War Petitions Collection, MSB 698, 1(1).

p. 79, C.J. Bosman (Greenpoint, 22.5.1901): Prisoner of War Petitions Collection, MSB 698, 1(1).

p. 80, R.S. de Vries (*Bavarian*, 19.1.1901): Prisoner of War Petitions Collection, MSB 698, 1(2).

p. 81, envelope addressed to S.P.J. van Zyl (Vereeniging, 21.6.1900): Eric Rosenthal Anglo-Boer War Collection, MSB 969, 1(8).

p. 82, D.J. Viljoen (22.4.1901): D.J. Viljoen Collection, MSB 655, 1(2). Quotation on Viljoen from the *Dictionary of South African Biography* IV, 743.

p. 84, B.A. & A.M. Lourens (Hijdelberg Tvl., 20.10.1900): H.C. Hopkins Collection, MSB 76, 12(18).

p. 85, F. Geldenhuis (Honengspruit, 25.3.1901): H.C. Hopkins Collection, MSC 76, 12(18).

p. 86, R.B. Pott (31.12.1900): R.B. Pott Collection, MSB 390, 1(1) pp. 217-218.

p. 88, A.S. Schabort (7.11.1901): A.S. Schabort Collection, MSB 437, 1(1) pp. 1-7.

p. 91, Jacoba Lorentz (23.7.1901): Jacoba Lorentz Collection, MSB 964, 1(1). Proclamation quoted from S.B. Spies, *Methods of Barbarism?* (Cape Town: Human & Rousseau, 1977), p. 129.

p 94, Jacoba Lorentz (22.7.1901): Jacoba Lorentz Collection , MSB 964, 1(1).

THE VICTORS (1901)

p. 98, J.B. Jardine (Burntop, Swazi border, 2.3.1901): J.B. Jardine Collection, MSB 272, 1(1) pp. 104-111.

p. 104, B.J. Jones (Pleasant Gift, 31.7.1901): B.J. Jones Collection, MSB 263, 1(1) pp. 152-156. Quotation on Rundle from *Times History* V, 444.

p. 106, R.B. Pott (13.2.1901): R.B. Pott Collection, MSB 390, 1(1) pp. 245-247.

p. 108, Leslie Fortescue (Transvaal, 11.9.1901): Leslie Fortescue Collection, MSB 187, 1(1). Quotation on Western Transvaal from *Times History* V, 495.

p. 112, M.W. Tyler (15.8.1901): M.W. Tyler Collection, MSB 496, 1(3).

p. 113, James Bell (63 Blockhouse, 15.12.1901): James Bell Collection, MSB 593, 1(1).

THE WAR PROTRACTED (1900-1902)

p. 116, Magistrate, Graaff Reinet (1.5.1900): W.P. Schreiner Collection, MSC 27, 2(371). Quotation on Walter Rubidge from *Men of the Times* (*Cape Colony and O.R.C. edition*) (1906), p. 508.

p. 117, M. van Huysteen (Krakeel River, 21.9.1900): Searle Family Collection, MSC 50,7(3).

p. 118, Henry Theron (Fraserburg, 9.8.1900): Earp Family Collection, MSC 47,4(1).

p. 119, Errol Earp ('Fair View', Rondebosch, 17.10.1900): Earp Family Collection, MSC 47,4(1).

p. 121, Thomas Searle (Great Brak River, 24.9.1901): Searle Family Collection, MSC 50, 22(6). J.W. Robinson quoted from letter dated 19.9.1901.

p. 122, C.J. Terblans (undated): Searle Family Collection, MSC 50, 22(6).

p. 123, Anonymous (20.9.1901): Searle Family Collection, MSC 50, 22(6). Description of the Theron Commando from *Boer army list, Cape Colony district* (*March 31st, 1902*), p. 125.

p. 125, Anna Kloppers ('Een droom'): Charles P. Hopkins Collection, MSB 929, 1(15).

p. 126, H.A.P. Soppitt (Stormburg, 28.11.1901): H.A.P. Soppitt Collection, MSB 679, 1(1).

p. 129, 'The treachery of Lilyfountain': Leliefontein Collection, MSB 446, 1(1). Copy of document and printed version both at MSC 39, 28(2). Quotation on Manie Maritz from *Dictionary of South African Biography* I, 513.

p. 133, P. Jacs Malan (Victoria House, Wellington, 2.9.1902): Methodist Church Collection, MSC 39, 28(2). Letter by J.G. Locke quoted from the *Methodist Churchman* (25.6.1902).

p. 134, J.G. Locke (29.4.1902): Methodist Church Collection, MSC 39, 28(2). Quotation from *Times History* V, 553.

THE END OF THE WAR (1902)

p. 138, A.C. Swinburne (The Pines, Putney Hill, 27.11.1901): Lord Henry de Villiers Collection, MSC 7,8(9).

p. 140, Chris Liebenberg (Buisfontein, 5.1.1902): Eric Rosenthal Anglo-Boer War Collection, MSB 969, 1(3).

p. 142, J.B. Jardine (Concordia, Namaqualand, 13.5.1902): J.B. Jardine Collection, MSB 272, 1(1), pp. 144-146.

p. 144, Jagersfontein burgher (undated): J.X. Merriman Collection, MSC 15,90(4).

p. 145, A.S. Schabort (Merebank camp): A.S. Schabort Collection, MSB 437, 1(1).

p. 146, R.B. Pott (19.7.1901): R.B. Pott Collection, MSB 390, 1(1), pp. 321-328.

p. 148, James Bell (39 Bree Street, Cape Town, 4.8.1902): James Bell Collection, MSB 593, 1(1).

WORKS CONSULTED

The following are the chief sources of information used in compiling the connecting texts in this anthology.

J.H. Breytenbach, *Die geskiedenis van die Tweede Vryheidsoorlog in Suid-Afrika, 1899-1902*; vols. I-VI (Pretoria: Staatsdrukker, 1971-96).

Boer Army List: Cape Colony district, March 31, 1901 (Cape Town: Intelligence Department, 1901).

Cape Times Weekly (1899-1902).

Diary of the Siege of Kimberley, during the Transvaal War, by a Beaconsfield Resident (Grahamstown: Grocott & Sherry, 1900).

A.M. Grundlingh, *Die 'Hendsoppers' en die 'Joiners': die rasionaal en verskynsel van verraad* (Pretoria: HAUM, 1979).

The Monthly Army List (1899-1902).

Bill Nasson, *Abraham Esau's War: a Black South African War in the Cape, 1899-1902* (Cambridge: Cambridge University Press, 1991).

Onze krijgs-officieren: album van portretten met levens-schetsen der Transvaalse generaals en kommandanten e.a. (Pretoria: Volksstem, 1904).

C.J. Scheepers Strydom, *Kaapland en die Tweede Vryheidsoorlog* (Kaapstad: Nasionale Pers, 1937).

The Siege of Ladysmith in 120 Pictures, from Photographs by Henry Kisch (London: George Newnes, 1900).

S.B. Spies, *Methods of Barbarism? Roberts and Kitchener and Civilians in the Boer Republics, January 1900-May 1902* (Cape Town: Human & Rousseau, 1977).

The Times History of the War in South Africa, 1899-1902; ed. L.S. Amery (London: Sampson, Low, Marston & Co., 1900-1909).

P.H.S. van Zyl, *Die helde-album: verhaal en foto's van aanvoerders en helde uit ons vryheidstryd* (Johannesburg: APB, 1944).

Peter Warwick, *Black People and the South African War, 1899-1902* (Cambridge: Cambridge University Press, 1983).

INDEX

illus: illustration (general)
port: portrait
All references are to page numbers.

bubonic plague, 82

Buller, Redvers, Sir, 31; (illus) 72

Burgher Peace Committee, 71

Burgher Scouts, 112

burning of houses, 67, 84, 105, 140; (illus) 87, 89

burning of veld, 105

Burntop, 98

Caledon River valley, 50

Calvinia, 127

camps (civilian population), 90-94, 100, 145; non-whites, 90, 140; (illus) 75

camps (prisoners of war), 76-90, 82, 85; (illus) 82, 137

Canada, 55, 116

Cape Colony: divided loyalties, 16-17, 21, 63-64, 116, 121-122; Boer invasion (1899), 17, 17-21, 62-63, (illus) 20; Boer invasion (1900), 73, 120-136, (illus) 115, 130. *See also* Cape rebels; martial law; Schreiner, W.P.

Cape rebels, 116, 121, 122, 124, 127; (illus) title page, 128; not highly regarded by Republicans, 143

Cape Town, 25, 54, 73-74, 76, 83, 148; (illus) 23, 43, 72. *See also* Green Point; Maitland; Simon's Town

card games, 108, 112

Carolina, 66

celebrations, 47-50 passim, 52, 72-73. *See also* demonstrations

cemeteries (military): (illus) 113

Ceylon (Sri Lanka), 76, 82; (illus) 82

Chamberlain, Joseph, 71

champagne, 31

Champley, Sister (Kroonstad): (illus) 75

Chrisp, Capt. (Petrusville): (port) 103

Christianity and the war, 22-24, 62-64. *See also* religious services

Christmas card (Green Point camp), 77

Christmas celebrations, 31, 46-47, 73

church services, *see* religious services

City of Cambridge (ship): (illus) 77

civilian population, *see* burning of houses; camps (civilian population); commandeering; denudation of countryside; looting; martial law; non-whites; women in wartime

Clements, R.A.P., 50, 51

club for officers (Ficksburg), 106-108

Coetzee, J.P.: (illus) 128

Cogle, Percy: (author) 54-56

Colenso, 10

Colesberg, 79

coloured people, *see* non-whites

commandeering, 14

Compies River, 102

concentration camps, *see* camps (civilian population)

Concordia, 128, 142-143

Cooper, Col. (Namaqualand), 135, 136

Cornelis River, 105

Coronation (1902), 148

Coster, Herman, 14, 15

Cradock, 124; (illus) 128, 144

Cronjé, Piet, 46, 47; (illus) 49

Cronwright-Schreiner, S.C.: 21, 21-22

cyclists, 121

Darling, 121

Davies, Lt. Col. (Sterkstroom): (author) 19-20

de Beer, P.J.: (author) 78-79

de la Rey, J.H., 110, 143, 148

De Langesdrift, 88, 105

de Villiers, Henry, Sir, 138

de Villiers, P. J.: (illus) 143

de Vries, R.G.: (author) 80

de Wet, C.R., 56, 69, 88, 108, 141, 148

demonstrations: pro-Boer, 116, 120, (illus) 117; pro-British, 25, 42, 72-73. *See also* celebrations

denudation of countryside (1900-1902), 66-67, 81, 84, 86-90, 98-106 passim, 113. *See*